ONLINE MARKETING BOOT CAMP

The Proven 10-Step Formula To:
Turn Your Passion Into A Profitable Business,
Create An Irresistible Brand Customers Will Love &
Master Traffic Once and For All!

by Gundi Gabrielle

First Edition Paperback: January 2020

ISBN: 9781654711597

The Cataloging-In-Publication Data is on file with the
Library of Congress.

*This is a **SassyZenGirl** Guide*

TABLE OF CONTENTS

Please Download the PDF Version

so you can access all tools and resources mentioned
throughout this book with direct links to each -
usually marked in bold throughout.

SassyZenGirl.com/OMBC-Resources

#ShareYourAWESOME!

#ShareYourAWESOME...

The deep, fundamental longing of every human being.

To matter.

To make a difference.

To be noticed and have an impact.

Everyone has that longing - even if deep down - and *everyone* has something unique and amazing to share!

I truly believe that.

Sadly, most people never get to express their AWESOME, never experience that deep sense of fulfillment, instead suffering through life stressed, financially strangled and feeling trapped in conditions they never wanted.

With seemingly no way out.

You may have tried a few online business options and some Facebook ads - or maybe you started a blog, but it's not going anywhere.

It's frustrating, exhausting and, frankly, annoying, because you really, really want to... - *need* to... - share.

But somehow...

You just can't cut through and reach an audience. Get your message heard and touch people.

Sound familiar...?

If you answered "yes", then I have good news for you!

Because, there *are* replicable systems and ways to make things happen, and they don't require a big budget or PhD to execute...:)

Knowledge is power and this little book will show you a practical, step-by-step plan for you to go from

ZERO to FULFILLMENT *(+ MUCHO BLING!!)* in the next 6-12 months!

NO Fluff or visualization exercises on the law of attraction *(though those can be helpful, too!)*...

Instead, practical advice that will not only show you what marketing methods will be best suited for your specific situation, but - *more importantly* - first lead you through the all important steps you need to complete, *before* even applying any marketing methods!

That's right!

You need to *first* get all your ducks in a row and *position yourself*, so potential readers and customers will *want* to hear and buy from you. In fact, be dying to!

That's... where you want to start!

If you do, you won't actually need all that much marketing later on, but can simply share what you have to offer with a hungry audience.

Doesn't that sound like a lot more fun?

Marketing *SassyZenGirl* style....:)

PART 1 of this book - *The 10 Sassy Questions* (= *the 10-Step Formula*) - will show you exactly how to do just that.

Once you have those 10 pillars in place - *and only then* - will we look at the 15 most effective marketing strategies to **take your brand from zero to awesome in the next few months**!

The good news:

If you apply the principles in this book, you won't be among the 98% of businesses and entrepreneurs that fail, but instead, finally have a path to success.

To reaching an audience and turning your passion, hobby or skill into a profitable business that can give you financial freedom long-term - *while* - also nurturing fulfillment at the same time.

The last part is especially important to me and part of the mission of *SassyZenGirl's* platform.

#ClaimYourFREEDOM® and *#ShareYourAWESOME*™ are our main taglines and while financial freedom is enormously important, it won't bring you peace and

happiness in the long run, if you don't also find a deep sense of fulfillment in what you do.

Make sense?

If it doesn't, no worries, then this is probably not the right book for you and you can always get a refund on Amazon within 30 days.

Yup....:)

I just offered you a refund on my book, because that's how I approach marketing and business.

I want people to enjoy what they purchase and find value in it.

A lot of readers seem to do so, considering 200,000+ downloads of *SassyZenGirl* books so far, while outranking every famous business author on Amazon along the way...

15. Gundi Gabrielle — Most Popular Books in Business & Investing
127 Home-Based Job & Business Ideas... | Passive Income Freedom: 23 Passive... | Kindle Bestseller Publishing (2019)... | Influencer Fast Track: From Zero to... | [BLOG] Starting a Successful Blog w...

16. Brené Brown — Most Popular Books in Business & Investing
Dare to Lead: Brave Work, Tough Con... | Daring Greatly: How the Courage to... | Rising Strong, How the Ability to R... | The Art of Asking: How I learned to... | Durf te leiden (Dutch Edition)

17. Robert T. Kiyosaki — Most Popular Books in Business & Investing
Rich Dad Poor Dad: What the Rich To... | Rich Dad's CASHFLOW Quadrant: Rich... | Rich Dad's Guide to investing: What... | Padre rico, Padre pobre (Nueva edic... | Rich Dad's Increase Your Financial...

But, of course, it's not for everyone, nor is it intended to be.

There is not a single product on the planet that will fit *everybody's* needs and expectations, and that's part of what we'll look at in the next chapter.

Nor do you need to come up with the next big, great idea to be successful as an online entrepreneur. Not at all...

So...

If the intro spoke to you and you haven't really reached the success and traction in your marketing that you had hoped for, this book will give you valuable pointers and a path to success.

If instead, you were looking for get-rich-quick hacks and tricks to make as much money as you possibly can without any regard for the people you are selling to, please - again - get that refund. No hard feelings...:)

Everybody else - let's strap in and get your marketing mojo into high gear!

Shall we...?

Chill with M

This may come as a shocker, but marketing - **the "*M-Word*" as I call it** - is actually really, really fun.

Yes, FUN!

Even for you introverts out there....:)

I'm one, too, by the way, and the internet is perfect for us solitary creatures, so no more "introvert excuses", *please...*

How can M be fun?

Seriously...?

Let me give you an example:

You just read an inspirational book that was really life changing and got you all powered up. Or you saw an absolutely amazing movie that you totally love.

What do you do?

You tell everyone you love, right...?.

Why?

Because you are so exuberant, that you just *have* to share and you want everyone to have that same, awesome feeling.

We've all done it - *right?*

Now...

Do you feel sleazy or pushy when you share in this way?

Is being an introvert a problem?

Nope..

Of course not, because your genuine enthusiasm will burst right through all that and keep you blissfully exhilarated - *dying to share*!

And you know what...?

That's really all good marketing ever is... *IF....*

You have your ducks in a row and positioned yourself correctly as I already mentioned.

That's why the *10 Sassy Questions* in the next chapter are so crucial to apply first, because with those 10 pillars in place, "marketing" will be so much easier, less expensive - and a lot of FUN!

On that note:

FUN and ADVENTURE are two important pillars at *SassyZenGirl* and also happen to be two of my main core values *(#1 being FREEDOM, of course)*.

Surprised me at first, but - *once realized* - totally changed how I approached my business and branding and has made all the difference in the company's success.

So...

Let's help you make "M" your friend and ally. A fun confidante that will take you from A to Z and not something dreaded, despised and avoided.

You pumped...?

PART 2 of this book will dive into the basics of copywriting and other must-have tools for your success, before we finally - in PART 3 - go over the 15 most effective methods to get your message across and your products sold.

Cool?

Obviously, there are many more strategies than just those 15, but I prefer to focus on *the most effective* strategies, so you can pick one or two to get started and *fast track* your progress, rather than getting bombarded with an endless list of this or that, leaving you more confused and overwhelmed than before.

Notice, I said *"one or two"* - and that's really all you need to become successful - and massively so.

Less is more and focus is everything!

...as we will see.

PART 3 will give you an overview over each strategy and then additional resources and training options to take things to the next level as each method has entire books and courses created that can go into much more depth than this short book.

Please understand:

To reach success with any of these strategies - and *start earning money quickly* - you need to learn from the very best. The top 1-2 % that have reached phenomenal ROIs and can show you their ninja hacks to fast track your progress. Good training is the one thing you should never skimp on, unless you want to waste years getting nowhere - which is what the other 98% do.

Don't worry if you are on a bootstrap budget!

I was, too, when I first started, and I found that to be a good thing in retrospect:

It's very easy to get carried away with amazing sales pitches and buy all kinds of expensive courses that you don't really need. Getting pulled in many different directions, but never getting anywhere.

When your funds are limited, _you are forced to FOCUS like nothing else!_ Picking one and really _making it happen_ - because you have to! You can't afford to dabble. You _have_ to get it done!

Most of the resources I share are either free or low priced - some are affiliate links _(always marked with a (*))_, but many are not - and they have been thoroughly vetted and tested.

Once you have decided on your marketing strategy of choice, you can quickly take things to the next level by learning to **_absolutely master and crush it_ with that one method**.

That... is the SECRET to fast - _legitimate_ - success on the internet. Months instead of years:

Pick ONE and focus on it exclusively with the best training you can afford - until you have _massive_ success.

That's it! - you are welcome...:)

The point of this guide is to help you:

#1 - Get your business set up the right way and position yourself for success

#2 - Learn marketing basics like copywriting, sales funnels and tribes

#3 - Pick the 1 or 2 marketing strategies that will be *most effective for your particular situation and business* + the best training resources to become successful with them quickly and efficiently.

Sound good?

Then let's rock it with the ***10 Sassy Questions***:

Part 1

The 10 Sassy Questions

Third time's a charm...:) - *so let me say it one more time*:

Before you look into any marketing strategies, be sure to answer the following 10 questions and make adjustments where needed.

These will be your 10 foundation blocks.

The pillars every successful business is built on.

Unless you have them *all* in place, your marketing campaigns will fail - and so will your business.

Don't worry...they are fun...:) - and will probably give you quite a make-over for your existing brand if you already have one.

Or...

An inspiring starting point if you are about to begin your entrepreneurial journey.

Ready?

Then....let's ROCK!

1 - *What problem do you solve?*

This.... is the most important question of all, so spend ample time on the big P as everything else will build on it.

To put it bluntly:

Customers, readers or followers are not interested in a list of features or - sorry...:) - you. At least not initially.

After all, they don't know you, and they get bombarded with offers all day long and are usually quite jaded by the time they see your stuff.

What *will* get their attention and make sales pretty much a self-runner, is when whatever you offer solves an *urgent* problem or need for them.

The more urgent, the easier your marketing will be.

So...

Your product or service should always be *the best* possible solution to an existing problem!

A REALLY BIG problem, pain point or frustration. Something your folks are thinking of constantly.

Vitamin vs. Painkiller

Anthony Grove in **this excellent Medium article** brought up the concept of products as:

PAINKILLER = NEED to have

vs.

VITAMIN = Nice to have

98% of businesses fail in large part, because they provide "vitamins" instead of "painkillers".

So before anything else, before even starting your business or thinking of a marketing plan, set yourself up for the low-hanging fruit - *especially* if you are brand new and don't have a large budget (or no budget!).

Start with:

What problem can I solve?

Ideally, a problem you have faced yourself.

And remember:

The world does not need more products!

But it can always use ***better solutions*** for existing problems.

See how that is a very different approach?

And how your marketing suddenly became a lot easier (and less expensive)?

How your branding, messaging, product creation and customer interactions completely change when your main focus is on:

1) What are the most urgent problems customers in your niche complain about?

2) How can you provide the best possible solution to one of those problems - greatly improving on what's already available?

This applies to physical products as much as services, and, of course, information products, like books, courses, blogs, videos, podcasts, etc.

Once you have answered those two questions - and I will share in a moment how to do that quite easily - you need to also become clear on:

What is the POLAR opposite of that problem?

Clearly paint a picture and help your customers envision and *feel* what life will be like after they tried your solution.

That's really all there is to it.

In a nutshell... :)

#1 - Find the most urgent problem customers have
#2 - Provide the best solution, *far* improving on all existing options
#3 - Help hungry customers envision and *feel* what life will be like after they take up your offer.

That's it. Take a breath... and then let's look at:

SUPER QUICK IDEA FINDER

#1 - Read negative reviews of popular products and books in your niche (Amazon or whatever platform features your niche and products). Find the most common problems and complaints and fix them - either with content, a product or a service.

Focus mostly on 2 and 3 star reviews as they are usually written by people who really wanted to like the product, but were disappointed, rather than 1-stars which are often just nasty and vitriolic.

#2 - Crowdsourcing Platforms like Kickstarter. See what products in your niche receive funding easily - and which don't.

#3 - Check Trendhunter or **Trendwatching** for the top trending products at any given time, sorted by niche.

#4 - Check Buzzsumo for the most shared topics at any given time, sorted by social media platform.

#5 - <u>MUST HAVE!!</u> - Facebook Groups. Join niche relevant Facebook groups where your potential customers hang out and read comments. What are common themes and frustrations that keep coming up.

You can even post a question or survey and invite feedback.

- *"What's your biggest frustration with X?"*

- *"What would be your #1 Dream Product in X that you wished was available"*

- *"What would be the absolute greatest result you could look forward to? that would be totally amazing."*

and so on.

Also write down specific phrases they use, how they describe the issue, their frustration and what they would see as the most ideal outcome. Those will be great to use later in your sales copy.

Interact with people, so you become comfortable communicating with customers in your niche. See what they respond to and what not.

If you are brand new, spend time building strong relationships - even friendships - in these groups, and you will already have found your first customers.

And...

So importantly, people you can ask for feedback, offer test & reviewer copies, run ideas by, etc.:

Your own FREE Focus Group, basically - which is priceless!

Occasionally, someone **in our Facebook group** will then mention that they are "introverts" and so networking is not really something they do...

Mmhhh....

I have only one question for you - and keep in mind, I'm the ultimate recluse and introvert (though you would never guess it if you met me):

How much do you _want_ it?

That's really all there is to it. Do you want it - or not?

> *You can either make Excuses*
> *or....*
> *Make Money!*
> *You can't do both - your decision!*

The internet has made it so easy and unobtrusive to interact with people whom you will mostly never meet in person, that it's absurd to still hide away. You can always retreat when you want to, leave a group, block people and set boundaries.

Very easy to do!

It's called *"getting out of your comfort zone"* for a reason...:) - and every successful person had to do it at some point in their lives - usually many, many times.

I also found that many successful entrepreneurs are actually introverts and leveraged that tendency to their advantage.

There is a certain depth and intense focus that comes with introversion, so if anything - it's an asset!

Therefore...

Kick your excuses in the *butt* once and for all - and just...

Get - it - DONE!

The sooner you do, the faster you can succeed. Simple math!
Cool?

Ok... back to groups and how awesome they are:

When you interact, always do it in a non-pitchy way. Give first, be a valued, unselfish and generous member of the group that everyone knows. Help people, support the group.

Then, when you are ready, asking a few questions or posting a survey will be welcome and group members will be happy to help and support you - even become your first brand ambassadors.

Observing your potential customers in Facebook groups will also help you determine who your specific audience is. More on that in #7.

Reddit threads, Quora, blog comments and sometimes YouTube comments can also be helpful here though the easiest way to interact with others will be Facebook groups.

#6 - Surveys - obviously, if you already have a customer base and mailing list - ask them.

#7 - Google "Top Trends" in your Niche

#8 - Check Instagram and Pinterest for relevant keywords in your niche and see what products come up at the top.

#9 - What are the top influencers in your niche focused on? Look at their content and products, also affiliate offers. Check their social media and blog posts: Which posts get the most interaction (likes, shares and comments).

Compile a list of possible options as you explore. Is there an area within a highly popular topic that you could improve on or fill in the missing pieces?

If you create a fantastic product or piece of content that complements an influencer's offering perfectly, you can reach out and suggest they share it with their audience. More on connecting with influencers in a later chapter, but this is one of the easiest ways to get their attention: Create an awesome product or piece of content that will make them look good with their audience and provide massive value to them.

#10 - Once you have 3-4 possible options, you can list all of them in a Facebook Engagement Ad and ask people to choose which they would want the most (if any). Monitor comments and see how they respond. Same with your mailing list or social media following if you already have one - *or* - the above mentioned Facebook groups where your customers hang out.

2 - Why is this important to you?

"People don't buy what you do; they buy WHY you do it. And what you do simply proves what you believe" - Simon Sinek

Yes, the famous WHY....

Introducing one of the most important ingredients to long-term business success:

Building a loyal following and customer base.

Nurturing those relationships and constantly focusing on increasing your "tribe" - *as it's called in cyber cool.*

It is much easier to sell to someone who has bought from you at least once, who already knows you and likes your products... than acquiring a new customer.

That's a no-brainer pretty much.

Given the millions of companies and products available today, you need something more compelling to attract - *and keep* - people with your brand.

That's where your WHY comes in and your core values.

Shared values and experiences are incredibly powerful and inspiring.

If customers *feel connected with you* through shared values and ideas - or shared experiences - they are much more likely to stay loyal.

So...

You need to become clear on WHY you do what you do.

What happened to you that makes this so important to you? Stories are crucial here to draw people in and make it personal.

Financial freedom and living an awesome life is, of course, one very important reason - but hopefully not your only one.

If you are also on a "mission" to make life easier, inspire others and change the world even just a little - it will set you apart from the rest of the field and is *inspiring* for anyone doing business with you.

Your tagline will usually represent some of that WHY.

At *SassyZenGirl* it's #ShareYourAWESOME and #ClaimYourFREEDOM.

The reason I create books, courses, videos, etc., is to empower others to share their "awesome" with the world.

The one thing you came here to do, that no one else can do quite like you, that will make a difference in the lives of others.

SassyZenGirl stands for *finding, expressing - and monetizing* - that "awesomeness" into an abundant, *fulfilling* life. And then pay forward and help others do the same.

I know what it's like not to have financial security. To be confused by the online marketing jungle and where to even begin. I was lucky to find good guides early on that significantly fast tracked my progress and got me where I am today. Now I'm paying forward.

My products are meant to simplify the process, starting with the **"No CLUE"** series and continuing with the **"Influencer Fast Track"** series and

SassyZenGirl TV *(coming soon)*. And doing so in a fun, sassy and easy-to-understand way.

Our friendly Facebook group is another important feature that allows me to interact with readers directly, answer questions and let them connect with each other. **You are welcome to join**, by the way, at **SassyZenGirl.Group**.

Building a business and growing something awesome is certainly much easier when you don't have to go it alone, and our group is a whole lot of fun.

Now...

Can you see how this is suddenly all more compelling and specific than just another series of marketing books?

So...

Get people to connect with your WHY and "competition" won't be much of a factor anymore!
It is *that* powerful.

Your WHY makes you unique and those who connect with your WHY, won't look elsewhere, but will be happy and excited to be with you and your brand.

3 - Is there a large enough existing market and customer base?

May seem obvious, but did you really check?

Or just guess and hope for the best?

It's *crucial* that you are sure, because without enough customers => no sustainable business.

That simple.

You are in this for the long run, right?

So...

Let's start with this novel idea:

Competition is good!

Yes, you heard right. In fact, the more the better!!

A crowded market means that people are passionately interested in this niche and willing to spend a lot of money on it.

That's what you *want*!

Cutting through the maze and being heard and seen - even as a relative newcomer - is absolutely possible, but requires that you have all your ducks in a row - aka all *10 Sassy Questions* answered.

That alone - will already set you apart from most competitors as most never bother and just throw stuff out, hoping for the best.

You definitely want to start in an *overall* niche that is highly popular with hungry buyers.

To confirm, google so-called "buyer keywords" together with your main niche, for example:

Buy + niche or product
Discount + niche or product (or coupon code, etc.)

These words signal what is called "buyer intent", meaning people are looking to buy and not just looking for information.

This is crucial, because some niches are very popular, but people aren't willing to spend money on them. They just want to read articles, watch videos or get everything for free - and you obviously can't build a business that way.

You can also tell by the number of (recent) reviews. Highly popular niches will usually have thousands of reviews on places like Amazon and those are only a fraction of the people who actually bought.

In addition, always look at the top influencers in your chosen niche - bloggers, YouTubers, IGers, podcasters - and see how they monetize their platform.

What affiliate products do they recommend? Do they sell courses and ebooks? Do they create their own products? Maybe run a store on Shopify, Etsy or Amazon? What type of products do they sell? What seem to be their bestsellers?

Always keep in mind:

In order to monetize your passion, skill or hobby, you *need to be able to sell* products or services related to that niche. If people love the niche, but aren't willing to spend money on it, you will have a very hard time building a business there.

Make sense?

Finally, check **Google Trends** to see overall interest and - very importantly - consistent or rising interest!

Armed with all the goodies above, you will never again fall into the trap of *assuming* you know what people want, but instead thoroughly check and research that you have a winner on your hands, *before you create* any products or think about marketing.

You can also run a few test ads on Facebook targeting different demographics and interests and see if you get any takers.

4 - Within that larger market, what is a sub-niche that you could "dominate"? That you could become known for? Where people will eventually think of you first?

This is another biggie most people miss.

Too general, too broad.

Yes, you ideally want a very popular overall niche, but then you need to drill down.

The more rookie and bootstrap, the more specific you need to be.

Start with just one customer avatar (more on that in #7) and laser target all your content and products specifically to that small segment until you gain traction. As your business grows, you can go wider, but initially you want a super specific sub-niche that you can "dominate" with a small, but clearly defined customer base.

That way, you can create a complete portfolio of products - physical or digital - and cover all areas a customer could possibly want and need. Full one-stop service.

You might even be the first person to provide that whole set, which is also great for sales funnels, up-sells, etc.

Why?

- Because you will have far less competition.

- It will be much easier to focus your marketing efforts on a small segment of the market vs. millions.

- It will also be much less expensive, even with Facebook Ads. If you are on a bootstrap budget, a laser targeted niche is the way to go...

As long as it's a *marketable* one! - Once again, check buyer intent, etc.

Food for Thought:

Even if you have a big budget...

Start with a bootstrap mindset, so you don't waste loads of cash unnecessarily as many beginners do.

Always keep in mind:

It does *not* take a lot of money to be successful and create income streams on the internet - contrary to what you might have heard.

As I already mentioned, when your funds are limited you will often make better decisions, because you have to *focus* a lot more - and you are *hungry* for change!

So...

Bootstrap is cool - not a problem at all!

5 - How is your approach different/better than everyone else's?

In "marketing speak" this is called "UVP" = unique value proposition or "USP" = unique sales proposition.

Your elevator pitch that makes it a no-brainer for customers to choose you over everyone else.

Always focused on benefits for the customer, not a list of features.

Remember how we talked about creating "better solutions" rather than just another product?

That's your UVP.

How is your solution to an urgent problem better and more effective for the customer?

How will their life be different and what do *you* have that no one else can offer?

Aside from functionality, a part of your UVP can also include your WHY.

Is it more inspiring, fun and interesting? Maybe your brand is environmentally conscious or you donate part of your earnings to a charity related to your business.

Or you make products that are normally very expensive or exclusive affordable to a wider audience like **Warby Parker**:

"Warby Parker was founded with a rebellious spirit and a lofty objective: to offer designer eyewear at a revolutionary price, while leading the way for socially conscious businesses."

It could be your brand personality and style. Think of Apple's stylish designs and cool, elegant brand persona. Apple users wouldn't be caught dead with an "ugly" PC, even if it were a superior machine. Style matters to them and they will never buy anything other than a Mac.

Or maybe you have a unique pricing structure or design.

Don't force this or stress on getting it "right" in the beginning, but simply start the process:

START with something.

And have FUN with the journey!

Being an entrepreneur is a highly creative process - that's part of what I love about it so much, especially with **my musical background.**

Most importantly...

If *you* are having fun, so will everyone else and that's one of the most attractive features (and UVPs) for any customer!

So... make it a fun adventure as we say in Sassy Land...:) - and everything will flow a lot easier for everyone involved.

One more thing:

Your UVP and branding will probably go through a few evolutions as you are gradually finding your place in the online world.

That's normal and you don't want to rush this. Certainly give yourself that time.
But...

START with something!

Even if it's not finished or "perfect" yet.

You won't ever get there, if you don't start testing things out.

So...

Play with it, have fun, dig deeper. Get a feel and try different things until you gradually *find your groove*.

Your own authentic voice and brand.

In the meantime, also start answering the next question:

6 - *What's your brand style & personality?*

"Your brand is what people say about you when you are not in the room" - Jeff Bezos

This is one of the "funnest" parts in all of marketing: creating your brand.

For starters:

Your brand is *not* your logo, branding or product. Those are just outer reflections.

Instead, your brand is the ___perception and experience___ people have with your business.

Think of your brand as a person - what would its traits be?

Isn't that a lot more fun than sitting down, hammering out a mission statement and trying to pick the "right" color and font?

Don't get me started on all the cookie-cutter, goody two-shoes, booooring mission statements...

Ugh....

SO not inspiring. No wonder most businesses are struggling...

And while logo and outer branding are obviously important, they also often change over time - even with famous brands.

What does not change usually, is the brand's personality. What it stands for. **The <u>association</u> we have when we think of that brand**.

How it makes us *feel*.

Why are people spending absurd amounts of money just to carry around a brand name on their clothing or accessories. It's quite silly when you think about it and yet, most of us do it.

Why?
Because those brands make us *feel* awesome!

And there is nothing wrong with that.

So...

How does your brand/business make people *feel*?

How does your brand talk to people? Share ideas, improve the world around it?

This includes personal brands, of course. If you are a coach, consultant or influencer, you still want to think about your brand persona. How does the world perceive you - and notice you? How is that unique and unmistakable?

Again, when you are first starting out, give yourself time to find your brand personality. Test things, see how it feels, until you find your groove.

Something that *feels genuine*.

Authenticity is one of the most attractive assets a brand can have and really draws people in.

There is so much cookie-cutter, generic, trying to fit in, trying to please branding, all kinda looking and feeling the same - and pretty boring.... - that an authentic brand that is not trying to hide its uniqueness, but instead makes it a prominent feature,

is refreshing and bound to break through with great ease.
Authenticity is Queen!

A great way to connect with that authenticity is to define your 2-3 main core values.

What is most important to you - and how is that reflected in your business?

Again...

NO goody two-shoes responses, please!

Pick a "list of core values" on Google and follow your gut.

Which words do *really* excite you and give you goosebumps!

Such an awesome feeling!

NOT... - what people expect of you or what you think you *should* be saying.

SO - boring!

Be YOU! - Awesome, flawed, unique you, with all the quirks and oddities that we all have, that make us human and help people connect with us...
And...

(Hopefully) a great sense of humor to boot.

Yup - _those_ core values.

The real you.

Got it?

Remember, how FUN & ADVENTURE surprised me when I really followed the "Goosebump Factor", instead of "deciding"?

It was life changing - and _SO_ liberating!

Imagine how this book would sound without those two values? If I would stifle myself to normal business speak?

I probably would have stopped writing - bored to death...:)

And it's not forced. It allows me to be who I really am, express the way I like to talk and not take things so darn seriously all the time.

And - *total shocker* - ... quite a few people seem to enjoy this style and actually read more books in the series!

Not everyone, of course - and that's totally fine.

But by being genuine and authentic to who you really are...

And expressing that unique YOU with abandon and joy - liberated...

You will attract the "right" customers and followers who are in sync with you and your values and who want exactly *your* kind of brand (and product) - even if the competition is less expensive.

Wouldn't *that* be sassyliscious ...?

So get that core values list right now - just google it - and dive in. With joy and abandon!

Don't pick anything that doesn't give you *goosebumps* and makes you *smile* instantly!

If you want to dig a little deeper:

One of the best books I've read on this topic is **Evan Carmichael's "Your One Word"**.

It will be eye opening and inspire you to find *your* one word and build your whole business and branding around it.

While we are on the topic:

The following three books are considered among the top resources on branding, each covering a different aspect. You'll thank me later...:)

Primal Branding
Building a Story Brand
The Brand Gap

7 - *Who is your target customer/ audience?*

"The aim of marketing is to know and understand the customer so well that the product or service sells itself." - Peter Drucker

Yup... I'm going there...

The much be-talked "Customer Avatar".

Seems boring, but is actually quite entertaining and will make your marketing sooo much easier down the road.

Remember focus?

And what a phenomenal difference focus can make?

Picture this:

You found your amazing product and niche. You are solving an urgent problem and are clear about your why. You've done all that.

Now, you want to tell your best friend about it!
How do you go about it?

With a boring sales pitch, listing endless features, trying to "sell" to them?

Of course, not!

He/she is your friend, right?

You care about them.

You want them to have the best and because you are super excited about your product and consider it absolutely life-changing, you really, really, *really* want your friends to benefit from it, too.

Not miss out.

Isn't that what we do when we come across something amazing?

Either a product, a funny cat video, a book that changed our lives or an inspirational message?

When we are excited, we want to share with those we love. Want them to partake in the awesomeness and all the wonders that come with it.

What is the key ingredient here?

Enthusiasm!

Genuine enthusiasm.

We just can't sit still, we *have* to share it and because our friends can *feel* that our *emotions* are genuine - they catch fire, too, or are at least willing to listen and consider.

Purchasing decisions are subconscious.

"Buying decisions are to 95% driven by unconscious urges, the biggest of which is emotion."

Notice the quote used "urges and emotions", not talking points and product features, because that is key here.

Evoking that same enthusiasm and excitement in your customer/reader/follower and the belief that what you are offering will truly help them, is what successful marketing is all about.

And it starts with genuine care, just like you would care for a friend.

People are numb and jaded from sales pitches and marketing hooks, but touch their emotions, help them see and *feel* what their life could be like once they start using your product or service, and you can build lifelong relationships with customers who will come back to you again and again - and choose you over everyone else, even if you are more expensive.

Now....

In order to do that, you need to, of course, know who you are talking to!

Right...?

Is it some vague, random "customer" or do you have a very clear image of who you are addressing? How they behave, what things they like? What humor or stories they respond to, how you can best connect with them?

That's why having a specific image/persona of one typical customer - or several for different demographics - is so important.

If you already have a business, you can use an existing customer as your avatar.

If not, go into Facebook groups where your target audience hangs out and observe. See how they talk, what phrases they use, what they respond to best, what makes them tick (or laugh). Typical commonalities, etc.

Immerse yourself, get to know your audience/customers *really* well and then create 1-3 avatars that you will use to test all your marketing on.

Now, instead of writing or talking to the big void, you will write and talk to Sally, Peter or Daniel.

Can you see (and feel) how different that is?

How the way you talk instantly changes, depending on who you are talking *to*?

For starters, you can do a little mental experiment:

Think of a favorite product and then - in your mind - excitedly tell:

- *Your mom*
- *Your best friend*
- *A colleague*
- *The cashier at the supermarket*

All with great enthusiasm.
Will you talk to each in the same way?

Of course not! - And that's my point here.

The more you can tailor your communications specifically to the people you are trying to reach - even including typical phrases they use (for example, when complaining about a problem that keeps them up at night) - the more they will feel like you are talking directly to them.

That you "get" them.

They won't know why, but somehow you touch them at a deeper core.

They feel connected to you even if they just saw you or your product for the first time.

Something about you is different, more specific and it speaks to them. They can't put their finger on it, but it's there, and they *feel* very comfortable around you.

Now combine:

- *An awesome, new solution to an urgent need*

with

- *Communications that instantly make people feel connected to you*

and you can't help but sell.

Without ever actually "selling" or pitching!

How awesome is *that?*

You won't have to squirm, feel sleazy or be embarrassed, because you have to "market" and "sell".

No, instead you'll feel great, because you are helping people by giving them what they urgently need, and you share it in a way that is pleasant, comfortable - *and* - trustworthy.

People don't want a billion different options. Everyone is busy.

If you have what they want and you present it in a fun, pleasant (non-pushy) way, they'll be grateful and look no further.

That simple.

You're welcome...:)

8 - Where do they hang out/Where can you reach them?

An important part of getting to know your customer avatar - *and crucial for any effective marketing plan* - is finding out where and how you can connect with them.

If your audience is an older demographic who don't use Instagram, but you focus most of your marketing on the Gram - *you ain't connectin'*!

If you are creating heavy machinery and tools for guys and try marketing them on Pinterest, you'll probably not get as much traction. Put them on YouTube though, and it might be a completely different story.

Make sense?

So, a crucial part of getting to know your customers is knowing where they love to hang out and then find them there.

Facebook groups are pretty universal, but they don't usually allow any marketing and pitching. However, you *can* use them to ask your folks what platforms they love to hang out on the most.

Then go to those platforms, find the bigger influencers, see how they market and model after them.

Each platform will have its own specific rules and strategies and we'll cover them a little later in this book.

9 - What is your clear, simple, laser focused message that a customer can easily understand in 5 seconds or less?

No features - just benefits.

Simple, clear, concise.

Easy to remember, possibly even in a tagline.

This should be easy now that you have all your other pillars in place:

- *Your winning product idea*
- *Your WHY*
- *A highly marketable niche*
- *Your laser targeted sub-niche*
- *Your UVP*
- *Your brand personality*
- *Your customer Avatar*
- *Where you can connect with them*

Stay focused on 1-2 benefits, so they instantly understand:

- WHAT problem you are solving
- HOW their life will *feel* different
- WHY your solution is the best fit for them

Include your brand personality and keep it simple.

The more clear and concise, the better.

10 - What stories can you tell?

Nothing captures people's attention as much as stories. They might not remember your name, but they *will* remember your story. Again, refer back to:

Building a Story Brand
by Donald Miller

Definitely include stories, case studies and other real life examples whenever you can. It is so much more compelling and fun for a customer or reader.

Start building a portfolio of stories and constantly keep adding. You can never have too many stories.

The most important is, of course, your founder story and why you started your company, service, book, blog, etc.

If your story is typical for what many of your customers are going through, even better!

Much more convincing if you tested your solution first on yourself, found relief and then started sharing it with others.

More relatable - and also more interesting.

Helps you connect with your followers or customers beyond just the sale.

Shared beliefs and shared experiences are the foundation for building an engaged and passionate following which, as we will see in the next chapter, will be crucial in fast tracking your success and also making it sustainable...

Final Validation

Now that you have completed all this preparation, there is one more final step you need to complete *before* beginning any kind of product creation.

...and you might have to do it several times until you find a winner:

Your Final Validation!

During *The 10 Sassy Questions*, you already did quite a bit of validating. Mostly pre-validation, like when you checked:

- *Product reviews*
- *Influencer offerings*
- *Trend sites*
- *Buyer keywords*
- *Customer comments in Facebook group*

and probably quite a few more.

You were checking what's already performing well in your market, so you could improve on something that's working well vs. completely reinventing the wheel.

Low-hanging fruit an'all...

Now you need to make sure that the specific offer that crystallized for you throughout this process, will convert in the real world!

It probably will, but *never* assume that you know - or hope for the best!

That's for amateurs.

You need to be sure, because product creation can be a time intensive process (and sometimes cost intensive) and you don't want to waste your precious time on something no one will buy.

No-brainer, right...?

That's, by the way, how most businesses operate and why they don't succeed:

Guessing what people might want, putting something out there and hoping for the best...

Bad idea!

So...

How, then, can you validate?

Several options:

1) Pre-Sell:

Pre-sell your product idea to your target audience - *before* you create it!

For example, an online course or ecom product.

Either to an audience you already have or find potential targets in Facebook groups and your circle of acquaintances.

Let them know that this course or product will be available in a few months, but if they want to get in with a special Early Bird price, they can lock it in now.

Set a 5-Day time limit when the offer will go away and include a refund/money back guarantee.

You then create a landing and checkout page, so people can purchase, and if you get enough takers (at least around 15-20), you know you have a winner on your hands.

Otherwise, look to fine-tune, shift focus or get a different topic altogether.

Also, ask all those who didn't bite, why not...? You might be surprised at the answers and you might not even have to change all that much.

If they *do* buy, then potential customers just validated your product with their precious credit card - you can't get a more powerful seal of approval than that!

It's not a problem to refund them later, should you decide not to follow through. People understand that you need to test the market and will be happy to help with feedback.

2) Start a Crowdsourcing Campaign

Can give you a strong sense of popularity in a short amount of time.

Once again, people validate with their wallets.

3) Test with Facebook Ads

This works great with smaller products and also services, like done-for-you, freelancer, coaching & consulting.

Once again, create a landing page and see if people:

1) Click on the ad
= your offer sounds appealing enough to check it out

2) Click through to your offer from the landing page
= your landing page was well set up *(or not)*

That way, you know where to finetune if needed.

If you don't know what a landing page is and how to set it up, **this video will show you.**

With Facebook ads, you can also test ideas for podcasts, blogs or YouTube channels - even book ideas and covers.

Run several ad options concurrently at $5-10 per ad, also test out different audiences (demographics, interests, etc.) - though obviously *only one parameter at a time* - and get a sense of how people respond.

As mentioned in #1, you can also run engagement ads, if you are still deciding between several options, and let people choose which ones they like the most/would want most urgently.

One of the most famous examples of how important testing and validating can be, is Tim Ferriss's book **The 4-Hour Work Week** - which was NOT the title he had originally intended.

Hard to believe now, but it wasn't his 1st choice - or even his 2nd - shocking as that may be.

Back in those days, Tim tested 6 different titles with Google AdWords, including:

Broadband and White Sand
Millionaire Chameleon
The 4-Hour Work Week

To his great surprise, *The 4-Hour Work Week* turned out to be the big winner - and the rest is history, as they say.

He also tested different book covers by sneaking dust jackets onto books at the local Palo Alto Borders and watching people's reactions...

Now ask yourself:

Would this book have been such a massive success without that irresistible title?

The 4-Hour Work Week

I mean....who doesn't dream of *that?*

Probably not - and even though Tim was already a skillful and experienced marketer at the time, he still needed to test and validate to land on this once-in-a-decade smash hit winner.

And...

What's good enough for Tim, is certainly good enough for the rest of us...:)

Please refer to the Facebook Ads chapter for further resources if this is new to you.

❀ ❀ ❀ ❀ ❀ ❀ ❀ ❀ ❀

Whatever way you choose to validate, don't let it scare you off or fall into analysis paralysis.

The cool thing:

It won't be perfect!

Certainly not the first time and it doesn't have to be.

What's important is that you take that first step, even if your first idea turns out to be a dud.

Or your 2nd and 3rd...

It's really not a biggie and a totally normal process every entrepreneur and creator goes through.

No one hits it perfectly the first time, but the more you test and immerse yourself - *and get feedback each time (!)* - the closer you will get to that kickbutt, smash hit winner that's brewing inside you and can turn your fortunes around quickly and in amazing ways.

Life is about evolution and growth.

A year from now, you will have a very different perspective, and a year after that, even more so - especially if you kept at it.

So chill on getting it "perfect" and focus instead on:

Get started + keep moving!

Keep testing, keep improving and keep laser focus on the end goal while *also enjoying* the journey.

If a test bombs - GREAT! - You were smart and just saved yourself a ton of time, money and headaches and...

You are one step closer to where you need to be!

All a question of perspective!

If this is your first time, there is a good chance you may have to test out several different options - *but so what...?*

It's quick and painless - and then you KNOW!

I always loved Thomas Edison's attitude. It took him thousands of attempts over several years to finally discover the light bulb, but when people asked him how frustrating that must have been, he just smiled and said excitedly:

"I have not failed. I've just found 10,000 ways that won't work."

What a way to look at life!

Obviously, we are not talking thousands of attempts or years of testing, but keep with the spirit of Edison: **Welcome every "failure" as one step closer to your final success!**

...and your journey will be a lot more fun - and faster, too, because you won't waste so much time complaining and being impatient all the time...

Right...?

If you follow these steps and keep validating your ideas, you *will* eventually get there.

Sooner or later.

When your time is right.

As long as you keep moving and stop interrupting every 5 minutes, because you aren't rich yet...:)

> *It doesn't matter who has success the fastest,*
> *but who has success the longest,*
> *meaning for the rest of your life.*

As I say in my book **PASSIVE INCOME FREEDOM**.

And I've seen it over and over again.

It is usually not the quick breakouts that have long-lasting success, but those that had an iron determination and stuck with it no matter what!

Who understood that _this is a process_ and that **_as long as you keep moving,_** you cannot fail - you are still going full steam ahead!

Soo...

With that burst of inspiration:

GO FOR IT!!

Part 2
Your Secret Weapon & Other Must-Have's

Your Secret Weapon

"Focus is the Mother of Success - Laser-like Focus!"

as I said in my book **INFLUENCER FAST TRACK.**

So where, then, should you put your prime focus after passing through the *10 Sassy Questions*?

Especially in your first year?

Drumroll...

On growing a passionate, engaged, *loyal* following for your brand!

THE #1 most important thing of all!

Be it customers, readers, social media followers or subscribers, your following - your "tribe" - will be what separates you from a quickie fly-by-night venture and will allow you to build a sustainable business and brand that will survive throughout changes in the market as well as changes in your products and overall direction.

Yup!

Might not have been what you expected, but that's the big secret, and you can see it in every successful brand. Certainly the ones that have survived for many years.

Why is that your most important marketing strategy?

Several reasons:

- As we saw before: it is a lot easier (and cheaper) to market to someone who has already bought from you or even just subscribed to your mailing list, than constantly attracting brand new buyers/followers.

- Your ardent fans will be ready for you when you launch a new product. They will be your first reviewers, leave ardent testimonials and spread the word to their entire network.

- If you start building a community where your tribe gets to interact not only with you, but also with each other to form a vibrant **community**, you have really won the day.

- People start identifying with your brand. They are proud to show it and talk about it, and they will want to see you succeed and put out more content and products.

- Shared values are more powerful than any catchy marketing message and will keep your followers loyal and connected to your brand - even if you change products and platforms.

- With an engaged, passionate following, you are starting a movement and there are few things more inspiring for humans than being a part of something bigger than themselves. A mission. Something that makes a difference. And the snowball effect can be tremendous.

- By yourself, you can only do so much, but with the support of hundreds or thousands of like-minded followers, the sky is the limit and you can spread your brand and message in amazing ways.

That - is the secret of any successful brand.

And *that* - needs to be your prime focus at all times!

It's a Date...

To build that rapport and connection with your customers and followers, be generous!

Give a lot - for free. Not physical products so much, but certainly digital, like ebooks, cheatsheets, reports, videos, etc.

In the "**Psychology of Persuasion**" **chapter** we will talk about the powerful principle of reciprocity.

When you are generous and give a lot, people will feel almost obligated to return the favor in some way.

Not just through sales, but also in the many other ways you may need their help:

- *Brand ambassadors*
- *Reviews & testimonials*
- *Feedback & survey*
- *Support during launches*

I occasionally see hesitation with new entrepreneurs **in our group** to participate in free giveaways of their Kindle books.

They talk about ROI and that they don't see any and are missing the bigger picture.

Basically, they are stuck in a penny pinching mindset where making a few bucks on a book (that may not even come) is more important than introducing *thousands* of new potential readers and followers to their brand who might become long-term fans and buyers - *but...* might otherwise have never checked them out.

Here is a big shocker - write it down:

With digital products <u>*you never lose anything*</u> when you give them out for free!

Let that sink in...

You are not dealing with production, storage and shipping expenses. Digital products *don't cost you anything* once created! - that's the beauty of it!

This allows you to be generous and trigger the principle of reciprocity without losing a dime!

Totally awesome!!

So....

Please, get out of that poverty, penny pinching mindset. Stop worrying about giving things away for free and focus instead *exclusively* on building a loyal, passionate following that can sustain and grow your brand for years to come!

When you are new, *your main objective needs to be to grow that quality customer base*.

Not the biggest, but the most engaged and the most loyal - and for that **you need to make an effort**:

Building a following is a lot like dating. You have to be patient, you have to woo. You make presents, you start a conversation and you slowly build a relationship of trust and mutual appreciation, so customers don't just come and go like one-night stands *(to stay with the dating example... :)*, but instead, grow into long-term, meaningful and productive relationships with your tribe.

Can you see how different - *and powerful* - that can be?

You don't need Millions...

Millions of followers, customers or readers that is, to make a good, full-time living.

Kevin Kelly started the idea in 2008 in his blog post **"1,000 True Fans"**, which was later shared (and made famous) by Tim Ferriss in his book **"Tools of Titans"**.

The basic premise being:

"To be a successful creator you don't need millions. You don't need millions of dollars or millions of customers, millions of clients or millions of fans. To make a living as a craftsperson, photographer, musician, designer, author, animator, app maker, entrepreneur, or inventor you need only thousands of true fans.

A true fan is defined as a fan that will buy anything you produce. These diehard fans will drive 200 miles to see you sing; they will buy the hardback and paperback and audible versions of your book; they will purchase your next figurine sight unseen; they will pay for the "best-of" DVD version of your free YouTube channel; they will come to your chef's table once a month. If you have roughly a thousand true fans like this (also known as super fans), you can make a living — if you are content to make a living but not a fortune."

If 1,000 true fan customers each pay you $100 per year, you will be raking in a nifty $100K per year, which is certainly enough to make a good living.

Numbers may vary depending on your situation and pricing, but you get the basic idea.

This also highlights the fact that quality is *much* more important than quantity when it comes to building your tribe.

Yes, it looks impressive if you have 500,000 followers and if you want to get paid for endorsements or influencer shoutouts, these numbers definitely matter, but from a customer conversion perspective, they often don't. So you need to know what your priorities are.

In general - be it social media or your mailing list - a smaller, but die-hard, dedicated following will make you a *lot* more money than a 6 or 7 figure list of people that barely know your name and don't have much of a connection to you.

So chill on the numbers...:) - and instead focus on growing your customer base with care, getting to know them, building long-term relationships, likability and loyalty, rather than pitching everyone to death just to make a quick buck.

There are different schools of thought on this. Some (highly successful) marketers recommend getting as many subscribers as possible, bombard them with emails and offers and weed down to the ones that withstand the onslaught - and still don't unsubscribe.

Apparently, it works and people make a lot of money this way - one marketing colleague even telling me: if you don't have at least a 20% unsubscribe rate, you are not marketing hard enough...

For me, that's not how I want to do business and I prefer to be respectful of people's time and a spot in their inbox while building something of long-term value. My mailing list is highly responsive, both in "open- " and "click-through-rate" (CTR), and when I do share an offer, sales are usually excellent.

You have to decide which way works better for you as long as you keep your #1 Focus on:

Start building an audience as soon as possible - even long before your first product is launched!

The exceptions are algorithm driven platforms like Amazon, Etsy, or YouTube. Here, the platforms can generate immediate sales - and subscribers - *IF* - you learn how to leverage their algorithm to automate sales - and by extension, grow a following.

Either way, keep your focus on building that loyal following from day 1 and you are setting yourself up for long-term success and freedom.

Psychology of Persuasion

The gold standard book on this topic is **Robert Cialdini's: Influence - The Psychology of Persuasion** and I strongly recommend you read the full book as it will change your whole concept of marketing and copywriting.

In the book, Cialdini lays out 6 universal principles of persuasion. They are widely shared on the internet, so I will give you a brief overview here, but the book will go into much more depth:

#1- Reciprocity
Give first, be generous with your help, and customers will feel inclined to return the favor. It's basic human nature. Giving away lots of valuable information, answering questions and asking for feedback are powerful ways to quickly build a connection of trust and respect with new customers and will induce reciprocity and goodwill.

#2 - Consistency

Once you make a choice or commitment, stay consistent with those choices and behave accordingly.

#3 - Social Proof
Reviews, testimonials and endorsements will all serve to make customers more comfortable buying from you. Whenever we make buying decisions and aren't fully convinced yet, we tend to look for social cues - feedback from other clients or customers to bring us over the finish line.

#4 - Liking
Likability is a major factor in buying decisions. Customers are much more likely to buy from someone they like than a generic brand. That's why building rapport is so important, because that personal connection and genuine likability can make all the difference.

#5 - Authority
Being a known authority in your field will go a long way to convince people to buy from you, especially for information products like courses or ebooks. You have probably noticed on most websites the "As seen on" bar or a client list of famous brands. The more prestigious, the more likely customers are to do business with that company or influencer. "Bestselling Author" is another highly coveted title that puts you

in a different league and can instantly establish you as an authority, even if you are brand new to online marketing. **More on that here.**

#6 - Scarcity

We value things higher when they are scarce or of limited availability. You might have noticed that some online courses only open several times a year for a few days and otherwise remain closed with a waiting list. Or special offers with a 5-day countdown, just to name a few examples. Scarcity is one of the most powerful marketing tools and should definitely become part of your arsenal.

Copywriting Basics

Words that Sell

Words have Power!

Both emotionally and physiologically.

You might have noticed, how some words make you tense up, even give you a funny feeling in your stomach.

"Fear", "Uncertainty", "Debt", "Problem" or "War" are great examples. Just watch your body when you say them...

On the other hand, words like "Bliss", "Hope", "Joy" and "Freedom" can make your whole body feel expansive and grand. They stir an AWEsome feeling. Physically, as much as emotionally.

Words stimulate different Areas in your Brain

Scientific research has shown a correlation between words and the various areas of our brain, each triggering a different response and very much affecting our decision making.

That's why words are so important in advertising and that's why copywriters - especially those who write magazine headlines - are some of the highest paid professionals in the world.

Writers who know how to trigger specific emotions can easily influence their readers - without them ever realizing it...

The "right" choice of words can dramatically increase conversions - be it a sale, finding new followers on social media, readers for your blog posts, or attracting clients for your services.

The secret is to tap into your reader's emotions and to understand the underlying feeling each word evokes.

Let's look at a few examples **by copywriter Belinda Weaver** and observe how just a few word changes can make a dramatic difference:

An Offer

This discount is available until midnight on Friday.

vs.

This exclusive discount offer is only available until midnight.
Act now!

A Call to Action

Download the party plan e-guide and start planning your
next party.

vs.

Download this free party plan to discover 11 simple secrets to
hosting parties everyone raves about.

A Brochure Headline

Our new product is helping millions.

vs.

Revealed! The exciting breakthrough that is
helping millions … Can it help YOU, too?

Words can change your Brain

Did you know that *even a single word* can set your brain
to relax - or brace itself for stress?

The book *Words Can Change Your Brain: 12 Conversation Strategies to Build Trust, Resolve Conflict, and Increase Intimacy* describes how:

"A single word has the power to influence the expression of genes that regulate physical and emotional stress. Hearing positive words strengthens areas in our frontal lobes and activates the brain's cognitive functioning. But even a single negative word activates our amygdala, the region of our brain that processes fear. And in turn, releases stress-producing hormones that disrupt our brain's functioning."

You are probably also familiar with the water crystal experiments of Dr. Emoto famously featured in the movie *"What the Bleep do we know"*.

Our Decision-Making Process is largely based on Feeling, not Information

According to Dr. Frank Luntz, author of, "**Words that Work: It's not what you say, It's What People Hear**", the words that people hear affect their decision-making, and this process is largely based on *feeling* rather than information.

"80 percent of our life is emotion, and only 20 percent is intellect."

If you want to generate a reaction in your reader, you must dig into the emotional and psychological impact of the words you are using.

Injecting your text with "feeling" words like "cozy" instead of "small" or "colossal" instead of "large" can instantly trigger a vivid image in your reader's imagination.

Think about how you want someone to feel or what you want them to envision, and choose a word from that category.

Now let's look at 10 of the most influential words in the English language:

The 10 most influential Words in the English Language

#1 - YOU (or your name)
The word "You" works as a substitute for a person's name, and we immediately connect when we hear our name.

"Remember that a person's name is to that person the sweetest and most important sound in any language." ~ Dale Carnegie

A study conducted by **_The Institute for the Study of Child Development_** found that hearing or seeing our name activates specific parts of our brain, namely the prefrontal cortex, middle and superior temporal cortex.

People naturally pay more attention when their name is mentioned in correspondence or a conversation.

Of course, you can't mention a person's name all the time, especially in an article or book, so "You" is a good substitute with a similar effect.

Not surprisingly, "You" is the most commonly used word in online advertising.

#2 - VALUE

Closely connected to #1. Your readers, clients or customers are not interested in all the features and skills you may have to offer, but only in the one important question:

"What's in it for me?"

"Customers don't care about features and benefits. They only care about value and achieving their objectives." ~ Colleen Francis in ***Nonstop Sales Boom***.

The key to attracting followers, readers or customers is to clearly define what VALUE your writing or product has to them.

They are not interested in hearing about *your* marvelous product, but only how it improves *their* lives.

Write with that objective in mind - from *their* perspective. Be it an article, a sales letter or - most importantly - a headline.

#3 - FREE

Everyone loves FREE goodies. The power of this four-letter word cannot be overstated.

Dan Ariely featured a fascinating study in his book *Predictably Irrational - The Hidden Forces that Shape our Decisions*, where he examined a very unusual "battle" between Lindt chocolate truffles and Hershey's Kisses.

Initially, the kisses were offered at 1c and the truffles at 15c, about half their value at the time.

When consumers were asked to choose, 73% chose the truffle, because 15c was perceived a great bargain.

Next, both lowered their prices by 1c, leaving the kisses at 0 = FREE!

The results were startling:

69% now chose the free kisses, rather than the bargain of the truffle.

In other words, the power of free had a far greater attraction than even a great bargain!

Ariely points to loss aversion (our disdain for losing out on things) and our natural instinct to go after the "low-hanging fruit" as the main reasons with our obsession with "FREE".

#4 - BECAUSE

A well-known principle of human behavior says that when we ask someone to do us a favor, we will be more successful if we provide a reason. People simply like to have reasons for what they do.
Roberto Cialdini, Author of *"Influence"*

In 1977, Ellen Langer, a social psychologist and professor at Harvard University, conducted a study to test the impact of phrasing on people's willingness to let someone cut the line.

Here are the variations she used:

- *"Excuse me, I have five pages. May I use the Xerox machine?"*
- *"Excuse me, I have five pages. May I use the Xerox machine because I have to make some copies?"*
- *"Excuse me, I have five pages. May I use the Xerox machine because I'm in a rush?"*

While only 70% agreed to let her cut the line with the first phrase, upwards of 90% let her skip when she used either the second and third.

Giving people a reason to do something is very powerful. The surprising thing is that it doesn't even have to be a great reason as in this case.

#5 - NOW

"Now" encourages people to act. It creates a sense of urgency. Usually "now" is used as part of a call to action: "Shop now", "Act now", "Subscribe now".

Or with the implied meaning of scarcity: "Limited-time offer", "Only 1 spot left".

#6 - INSTANTLY

Similarly, immediate words like "instantly" trigger mid-brain activity and feed our desire for "instant" gratification.

If we can access something immediately, our brain jumps on it like a shark.

#7 - EASY

We all like things to be easy and quick. Adding this word in a headline or sales copy, releases a lot of resistance, because....what can go wrong. It's easy, right?

#8 - SECRET

In a similar vein, offering a "secret tip" or "secret strategy", feels like a shortcut. And we all love things easy!

The word "Secret" also evokes a sense of exclusivity, or belonging - one of our most primal urges. We all love to be special, be part of a special group and have access to tools and information that are reserved only for a special few.

The word "secret" in a headline peaks your reader's interest, because none of us want to be left out. We want to be on the "in" of things. The "smart" people who know stuff.

#9 - SURPRISING

Similar to "Secret" without the exclusivity. "Surprising" churns our curiosity. We *have* to know, it's irresistible. And we'll likely click on that headline, just to find out - or be left wondering for the rest of the day....

#10 - IMAGINE

This is a big one for tapping into people's emotions and feelings. Visualizing the result your article, book, product or service will bring to a reader is incredibly powerful.

Rather than focusing on features, you once again tap into the "What's in it for me?" question that's on every customer's mind.

Once they start to *feel and live* what your solution can offer them, they are much more open to hear more.

There you have it.... 10 of the most influential words in the English language.

Power Words

Another must-have tool in your copywriting arsenal!

Power words allow you to tap into and deeply stir your reader's emotions. Buying decisions are mostly emotional, so incorporating power words into your sales copy - and very importantly, into your headlines and titles - is crucial.

Here is an expansive list of 401+ Power Words - grouped by emotion.

Add a few in your headlines and sprinkle some throughout your text, and you will be amazed at how much better your readers will respond.

Headline Hacks

The most important area of copywriting - and your entire marketing - will be headlines and titles.

It's an extensive topic that goes beyond the scope of this book, but here is **one of the best (free) in-depth guides by Jon Morrow**, one of the most successful bloggers and marketers of our time was editor of Copyblogger for several years, before launching his own 8-figure blog (yes, 8 figures annually!) *Smartblogger.*

In the report, Jon shares the best performing headline templates as well as the psychology behind them. Studying this guide will be one of the best things you can ever do for your business as titles are one of the main factors to get people in the door and interested initially.

Irresistible headlines are a must-have to cut through the maze of massive competition and this guide will be a valuable reference from here on out. No need to reinvent the wheel, you can use what has worked for decades and tailor it to your specific needs and audience:

52 Headline Hacks(*)
A "cheat sheet" for writing blog posts that go viral!

SassyZenGirl.com/Headline-Hacks

Call To Action

Last but certainly not least, you need a closer:

Your CTA or "Call to Action".

The simplest form can be:

BUY NOW

CLICK HERE

LEARN MORE

CTAs prove another phenomenon of human psychology:

That people are a lot more likely to complete an action if you tell them to do so.

Even when the "command" is obvious.

It's a subliminal trigger you never want to leave out that needs to become a part of any ad or sales copy.

If possible, multiple times.

Rather than the generic versions above, this is a great time to get creative and show off your brand's personality.

Sales Funnels

What is a funnel?

Excellent question! - and a crucial one for understanding how successful online marketing works.

A sales funnel is a chain of products that lead a customer through your brand and products with the least resistance.

In fact, sales funnels often start with a free product.

#1 - FREE LEAD MAGNET

If you include a free offer, also called a "Lead Magnet" (free cheat sheet, checklist) at the beginning of your funnel to get subscribers onto your mailing list, this will be part 1 of your funnel.

Why?

Because it shows commitment from this customer to at least hand over their coveted email address, which people are usually very reluctant to do. Your offer and presentation must have been appealing enough for them to make this trade and if they like your freebie, they are much more likely now to pay for your next offer, because they are now convinced that you can provide what they need and know what to expect.

No more pitching or clever sales copy needed!

Give a free taste, provide *awesome* value and then offer more.

That's how *simple* smart marketing really is!

Once new subscribers are on your list, you can build a relationship with them and introduce them to other, higher priced products. Or...

Offer what's called a "tripwire" on the Thank You page.

#2 - TRIPWIRE

A tripwire is the next step in your sales funnel and usually a low-priced product in the $7 range.

While the price may seem low, this sale is crucial!

Why?

Because sales psychology tells us that once someone buys from us - even at a very low price - they are now much more likely to also buy higher priced items.

The initial barrier is gone. That difficult first sale has been converted. From now on, things will be a lot easier.

From there you can go to:

#3 - A CORE PRODUCT (or several).
Something in a medium price range, anywhere from $27 to $297 depending on your niche and topic.
Please note: pricing varies greatly between niches, and these are just rough numbers to give you an idea.

#4 - A PREMIUM PRODUCT
In the $497 to $1997 range (or higher in some niches) - again, not limited to just one.
Core and premium products can include online courses, but also services, coaching, consulting, and any other products.

UPSELL MAGIC

McDonald's were among the first to use upsells as a regular marketing and sales practice. When someone buys a burger, the cashier will always ask:

Do you want fries with that? or a Coke?

Upsells is where the magic happens. Where you can turn a low-priced initial product into a big overall sale.

Successful ecommerce entrepreneurs use this technique to easily triple and quadruple their revenue per campaign, even on "Free, Plus Shipping" offers.

Upsells are often combined with scarcity, usually a time limit of a few minutes by which you can buy at a special discount or lose it forever.

As we all know - it works... :)

And it works just as well for information products like ebooks and courses.

How to be Seen

You become financially free by owning traffic - Russell Brunson

Before we dive into specific traffic strategies, let's clarify some logistics and terminology.

To sell anything online, you need to bring customers to your offer.

That's called "driving traffic".

There are several different types of traffic and you will eventually use a combination of all:

Organic Traffic
Free traffic, usually a result of search engine traffic or OPA.

1) Google, Amazon, Youtube, Pinterest, Etsy and the like are all search engines, meaning users find what

they are looking for by entering a search phrase (= keyword) and the platform's search algorithm will deliver what it considers the best suited, most relevant results.

Each platform works differently and uses a different set of parameters to decide what it considers relevant and who shows up at the top.

To generate organic, free traffic on any of these platforms you need to dive deep and fully understand how they work and what you need to do to get your brand showing up in the top spots.

Don't worry, it's not complicated, but there is a learning curve with each and also some testing until you hit the sweet spot.

To show you how important this is:

On Google, the #1 spot usually receives about 32% of all search engine traffic - which is huge!

#2 and #3 get about 25% and 19% respectively.

After that, the numbers go down dramatically, with page 2 already being referred to as the "graveyard" among SEOs *with less than 1%(!)* of clicks!

2) Another form of organic traffic can come from your social media platforms. If you have an engaged following on, let's say, Instagram or Facebook, you can occasionally send them to your offer - free and easy.

3) If a peer, influencer or niche relevant institution gives you a free shoutout or - *even better* - lists you permanently in their *"Recommended Resources"* section, that, too, is free organic traffic.

Evergreen Traffic
Which brings us to a sub-form of organic traffic, called "evergreen" traffic, meaning traffic that keeps on coming without specific events or effort.

Search engine traffic can become mostly evergreen if you set it up right and built enough authority on each platform (don't worry, we'll get into more detail in the coming chapters).

My books on Amazon for example drive evergreen traffic to all my other ventures and have generated me an easy 6 figure passive income, going on 7 now - all while traveling the world and mostly living a **4-Hour Work Week**.

Top ranking in Google, YouTube or Pinterest can have a similar effect as we will see.

If your product is listed under "Recommended Resources" on an influencer or institution website - or in a bestselling book - that, too, can generate an abundance of evergreen traffic - completely free and you don't have to do a thing.

As opposed to shoutouts and social media posts, which can provide temporary bursts, but they are not evergreen.

In the coming chapters we will see a few more options for evergreen, so stay tuned...

Paid Traffic
Finally, there is paid traffic. No explanation needed here. Examples are:

- Ads
- Paid Shoutouts
- SEO *(depending on what method you use)*
- Media Outreach *(= hiring a PR firm to get featured in major publications)*

A word of warning:

As we now go into 15 highly effective marketing strategies, please remember:

Focus is everything!

Pick ONE - *and only one* - for the first few months and absolutely master it.

In some cases, two can go together, for example: a blog as your main platform and one of the other strategies to generate traffic to that blog, like Pinterest or SEO. Even then, pick only ONE of those additional methods until you achieve *massive* results.

I say "massive" for a reason:

When you focus on *one* marketing strategy fully and exclusively until you really master it, the results can dramatically sky-rocket your income in a pretty short amount of time.

This will definitely not happen if you pick three, four - or even more! Same goes for multiple platforms.

Yes, we can all multi-task, but we are *much* better and more efficient when we focus on just *one* thing at a time - and one thing only.

One of the biggest mistakes most entrepreneurs (and not just newbies) make is trying to be everywhere and cover everything:

All the social platforms, a blog, a podcast, maybe even a YouTube channel - with the sad result that nothing really gains any traction and they are still struggling to make a few bucks years later.

Please understand and *really* let it sink in:

It only takes ONE traffic source to bring you a six figure income and even financial freedom - but *only* if you *fully* master and leverage it.

That will take all of your time and attention for the first few months, so please use your time wisely.

Once that one traffic source is established and running well....

Once you generate a consistent stream of income from that one source...

Definitely add another and eventually even a third, because you never want to keep all your eggs in one basket. Platforms change and shut down all the time, so you never want to rely on just one, but...

In the beginning, you need to focus on ONE ONLY until you start generating consistently great results.

So, yes...

Definitely read through all the scrumptious options coming your way in the next few chapters and get a thorough overview.

But then...

Pick ONE!

And apply complete tunnel vision and laser focus until you achieve massive success!

Break through, be wildly successful - and then scale up and expand.

98% of new businesses fail - that is a sad truth.

If *you* want to be in the rare 2% that succeeds...

THIS - is how you do it!

Find and pick the marketing strategy that is best suited for your specific needs and personality and then:

Focus and master ONE.

That simple.

Alrighty?

And...

Get top level training from entrepreneurs who have achieved massive success with this one method and share their ninja hacks and strategies in a course or book as that will be the shortcut.

I will provide plenty of free and paid training resources as we go along, so let's now dive in and enjoy:

Part 3
TOP 15 MARKETING STRATEGIES

#1 - The Ultimate Fast Track Strategy!

I'm obviously a little biased... :) but in my experience, self-publishing *(of all things...)* has been the easiest and fastest way to:

- *Grow a following = Instant traffic right after publishing*

- *Gain instant authority (nothing beats the authority of a "Bestselling Author" title!)*

- *Leverage the massive OPA of the biggest market place on earth - Amazon! - which also makes up 70% of the book market.*

- *Build a trusted relationship with your readers and future customers in a completely non-salesy way.*

In addition:

- *You can easily include affiliate links and funnel your newfound traffic to any other project you want to grow: online courses, your blog, podcast or YouTube channel, your social media platforms, coaching & consulting services, Done-For-Your services, you name it!*

And - so important:

- Publishing can get you a massive success experience quickly, which is important in the beginning. There is nothing like seeing your name and book for the first time as a #1 Bestseller in the charts....

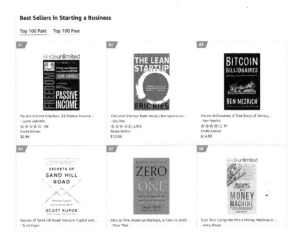

or with the coveted Bestseller badge...

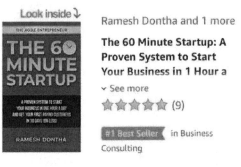

while....earning your first dollars online.

Which you *will*, if you follow **the SassyZenGirl method**.

Every time a new student in our **Facebook group** goes through that journey, it is life-changing for them and brings a huge boost in confidence and motivation.

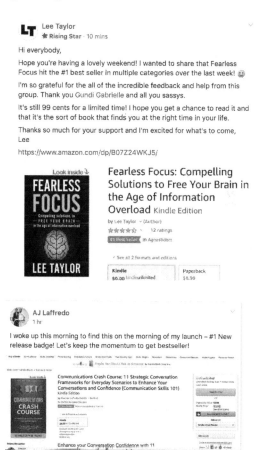

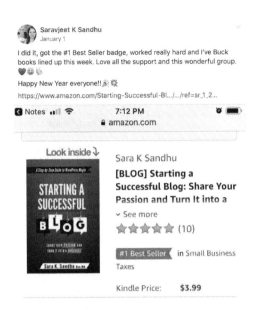

So starting with a bestseller launch before anything else, will be one of the most effective paths to jump start your online career and gain traction quickly.

And... - it's much easier than you might think!

If you think I'm full of it, no worries...:) - I know it's hard to believe at first.

Let's get some common myths and 'buts' out of the way, so you can stop wasting time and start with a bang, shall we...?

MYTH #1 - You need to land a "book deal"

Nope - you do NOT need a traditional publisher! And don't ever fall for the many - *ridiculously overpriced* - "publishing company" scams - or publishing coaches! You don't need them.

It's become a rampant industry, trying to trick you into paying *them* thousands of dollars for services you can easily do yourself at a small fraction.

Please understand, a legitimate publishing company will *never* ask you to pay them, but rather, will pay *you* an advance, plus royalties.

And, yes, I said "easily", because publishing a bestseller on Amazon is really not that complicated at all!

Why?

Because Amazon has thousands of sub-categories, each with its own bestseller list, so all you have to do, is be #1 in one of those small sub-categories and you are a "#1 **Bestselling Author**".

Often it only takes a handful of sales per day, which can easily be achieved if you apply a few simple strategies.

Sassy WOW!

To make it even easier, **this FREE book** will show you exactly how to do it from A to Z - every single step. Follow that and you will join the thousands of first-time authors around the world who have reached #1 Bestselling Author status, often in as little as 30-90 Days!

Get it free at **BestsellerPublishing.net**.

Also, you probably didn't know this, but....

Traditional publishers expect you to *already have* a huge following and will expect *you* to do most of the marketing. Since most authors don't know how to market, the publishing houses will send them to the self-publishing industry to learn how. I'm not kidding...

All the while, they *own* your book, have complete control over it, royalties are a pittance and it takes many months to finally get published.

Most importantly, you are restricted in using your book to market your business (lead magnets, sales funnels, affiliate sales - forget it!)

So, unless you are a well-established authority already and someone offers you a 6-figure advance, stay away from traditional publishers!

 Cathy Anderson Corn 🎗 Hey Gundi Gabrielle, this comes after over 25 years of knocking at the door of traditional publsihing. I would go to a writers" conference and have a pitch session with an agent or editor and come home crying. After all the heartache, this is totally amazing and unbelievable. Your book and Amazon KDP have given me my minutes in the sun. My gratitude journal is full of your name and I hope you are having a great day!

Like · Reply · 35m

MYTH #2 - It takes years to write a book

Nope! - Kindle books are short and online readers prefer shorter content. 10K-25K words is a good range for well-performing books. That's basically a really long blog post, so certainly possible to get done on the side in a few weeks.

Instead, it is smarter to split a topic into 3-5 sub-topics and publish a series.

Writing 1 book on a topic you know really well, shouldn't take you more than 2-3 weeks. It's mostly sorting what you want to say, chapters and sub-chapters and then fleshing out a first draft.

Publishing a successful book in 30-90 days is absolutely possible and many of my students have done just that and reached #1 with their very first book! - often outranking famous authors.

MYTH #3 - You need a large following already

Triple NOPE! - in fact, it's the other way around. Because of Amazon's enormous reach, a successful book can ***instantly* jump start your following** and bring you hundreds of new followers in the first month alone.

Even as a complete internet newbie with no clue about marketing! *(although **after reading the above book**, you'll be a book marketing ninja in no time!)*

That's why I suggest ***publishing a book first, to jump start your traffic*** and online following while instantly gaining prestige and authority as a bestselling author.

There is no other method as effective - *and simple* - not even close!

MYTH #4 - Book marketing is a full-time job + you need lots of experience

Noooope! - **Again, read this free book** and you will know everything you need to publish your first #1 Bestseller (non-fiction)!

If you apply the principles taught there - and don't cherry pick...:) - Amazon's algorithm will keep your book selling for you - long-term. No further marketing needed.

I know, that sounds too good to be true, but I've done it 13 times and thousands of my students around the world have done it as first-time authors, so there is no need to make things difficult or complicated, just follow those simple steps and see your book in that spot:

You can probably imagine how *awesome* that will feel, right...?

So...

Get that out of the way. Publish your first bestseller, make your first dollars online, get the prestige and pedigree of a "Bestselling Author" - and then expand into whatever else you want to do in your business journey.

Publishing should be the *beginning*, not the end of it.

But it will be one heck of a start!

To be clear - we are not using any scam tactics - none whatsoever! Everything taught is fully in line with Amazon and KDP TOS. Understand the platform and how to leverage its power, and you won't need to cheat to be successful.

Instead, you can build a business with customers and followers who respect you and *want* to hear from you.

You didn't expect that from the M-Word, did ya...?

The best part...

Self-publishing is one of the most passive ways to run a business and does not require me to constantly create and post new content as you will have to with any other content platform, be it social media, Youtube, Blogging or podcasting.

I'm not the most consistent person and I need breaks in between. I tend to have highly creative and active phases alternating with lots of chill and laid back where I'll binge watch favorite shows and movies, take road trips or just enjoy life.

For me, that's the whole point. To finally have that freedom to take time off when I want to, live a **4-Hour Work Week** and then dive back in full steam when inspiration and creativity kick in.

Publishing is the only platform I know that allows me to do that with such freedom - while building a 6-7 figure passive income business around it, in my case with online courses and affiliate marketing.

It's the easiest and fastest way to get a consistent stream of new leads and traffic - if - you learn how to get Amazon to keep selling your books *for* you and promoting them long after the initial launch is over.

Then you just keep publishing a new book once in a while - and you are done.

Alrighty....)

On to more fun marketing strategies:

#2 - Influencer Bonanza

Yesss....Influencer marketing!

The big, glam "I"...

Not just a pretty word, but one of the absolute powerhouses of online marketing, catapulting thousands of new businesses to 6, 7 and even 8 figures in a short amount of time!

Influencer marketing, and specifically influencer shoutouts can become one of the most effective and fastest ways to drive massive traffic - and sales - to your brand.

Success depends on two main factors and you need both in place or you will just be wasting money:

#1 - The "right" influencers

#2 - All *your* ducks in a row! - Meaning, a high-in-demand product and an awesome ad with amazing footage (photo or video) and great sales copy. Same goes for any landing pages or other marketing material in your funnel.

To give you an idea of how amazingly well influencer shoutouts can work, check out **this video by "High on Life" where they grow a travel Instagram page by 100K followers in 48 hours**!

This is, of course, an extreme example and worked in part, because *High on Life* was already well connected with most of these influencers and knew who to use and how.

But more importantly, it also worked, because they had an *amazing* video ad!

Great footage, fast cuts, great music - totally awesome and definitely highly appealing to the intended target audience.

Replace that ad with a generic photo and a cutsie text and all the influencers in the world couldn't rescue it! It would just be another wannabe influencer, pretty, but generic. No reason to make the effort and hit that follow button - let alone tag others and share it.

That... is what a lot of people miss and then fail with influencer marketing.

You can't just quickly throw something together and hope to get rave responses - especially on Instagram!

Your ad needs to be professional looking and jaw dropping. Viral potential, ideally.

The better your ad, the better the results - *by far* - so definitely a worthwhile investment to get it professionally edited and designed.

Even if you are not ready for shoutouts just yet, start by getting to know the scene and who could eventually become a good partner. These things take time and the sooner you start, the better.

Which brings me to #1 - the "right" influencers and how to find them:

1) Find out where your customers / target audience mostly hang out -   Instagram, Youtube, Blogs, Facebook, etc.

Next, subscribe/follow 10-20 of the top influencers in your niche and check their content regularly. See what ads they run and how well their audience responds to ads (number of comments, views).

Are they passionately engaged and recommending this product, tagging their friends, sharing, etc.? Or are ads usually the posts that get ignored.

You will quickly notice that some audiences respond better than others and you (obviously) want to focus on those who do.

Follow both micro & macro influencers. "Micro" is usually defined as <100K followers on Instagram and <250K followers on Youtube and Facebook.

Micro-influencers will usually be a better target for you in the beginning, because their rates will be lower (or even free in return for product samples) and their audience is usually a lot more engaged and connected with that influencer.

Meaning, they will follow their advice or recommendations to the letter vs. a more loose connection that bigger influencers or celebrities tend to have with their audience.

There is no perfect rule obviously and every niche will be different, but this is a basic guideline to get started.

Additional ways to find suitable influencers:

- Ask your customers or audience who *they* follow (and start following them)

- Who do your competitors work with (or companies with overlapping audiences, even if your products are different)?

- Check popular hashtags and see what influencers keep showing up in the top spots

- Check Instagram recommendations and start monitoring their ad activity

- See who your chosen influencers are following

- If you are a local business, see who local PR companies are working with

- Find influencers in your area/location

- Use platforms like **Heepsy**(*) to quickly narrow down by niche and audience engagement.

Once you have worked with several influencers and found a group that brought you good results, you can also book influencer "clusters". Meaning, you schedule them out over several days during a product launch to really build momentum and brand visibility.

Fans usually follow several influencers in the same niche. This way, they will keep seeing your product over and over again and eventually can't help but want to check it out and see what all the fuss is about.

Rates obviously vary greatly between niches and also Influencer level, anywhere from $10 per shoutout to 6 figures for major celebrities. If you have a great physical product, influencers will often be willing to give you a shoutout in return for a free sample. Certainly, micro influencers will, and they can start at just 5,000 followers.

Always remember, it's not so much about follower count, which can easily be faked, but about engagement.

Genuine engagement.

Easily detectable when you start reading comments. Fake/automated comments are always generic and easy to spot...

"Dope shot, bro"
"Keep up the good work"

Anyone...?

A page with a huge following, but almost no interaction (views, comments), is a dead giveaway for fake followers.

So...

A micro-influencer with a small, but highly engaged (real) following, who clearly has a connection to their audience and constantly interacts with them in the comments, will have a much better chance of success than a mostly dead page with 500,000 followers.

When partnering with an influencer, always be sure to have a clear, written agreement of what is expected:

- *Number of posts/stories and when to post*
- *Specific actions you want the influencer to perform*
    (demonstrate, review, unpack)
- *Photo or video*

If you already have a brand and platform in place, plus, a decent marketing budget, a platform like **Hey Influencer** can make things smooth and easy.

Founded by Gretta van Riel who built 4(!) multi million dollar ecomm businesses, mostly through influencer marketing, this platform connects thoroughly vetted influencers and brands, providing a safe platform where funds are held in escrow until all agreed actions are completed.

While Instagram is the best-known platform for influencer marketing, shoutouts can, of course, work wherever there is an influencer with an audience:

- *Bloggers*
- *Authors*
- *YouTubers*
- *Podcasters*
- *Facebook*
- *Twitter*
- *Pinterest*
- *LinkedIn*

The same principles apply. Find 10-20 top influencers, both micro and macro. Start following/subscribing them and see what products they endorse and - very importantly - how their audience responds. Once you narrow your list, contact them and ask if they do influencer shoutouts and what their rates/conditions are.

Influencer shoutouts can have a massive - instant - impact and are well worth the initial effort of finding and screening suitable partners.

Once again - be sure, you are ready. You don't want to pay for shoutouts when you are barely starting out and still finding your way. You want to present a compact, professional looking product and ad.

However, from Day 1....

Start following and locating suitable influencers, so you have a list ready when the time comes and can launch your first product with a bang (instead of crickets...:)

#3 - Collab OPA

What is *that*...?

OPA stands for leveraging "other people's audiences" and is the fastest way to grow online.

Whether you use platforms like Amazon or Youtube, influencer shoutouts or your peers, you will grow a lot faster if you tap into existing audiences than growing everything from scratch.

Influencer shoutouts are a paid form of OPA.

Peer collaborations and guesting are two *free* and highly effective methods of spreading your awesomeness quickly - even as a relative newbie.

Perfect for a bootstrap budget!

Once again, you want your ducks in a row. A highly marketable product, defined brand and message, and a website or other platform to send new leads to - ideally with a sales funnel in place.

Peer Collaborations

First of all, please stop seeing other entrepreneurs in your niche as competition.

Instead...

See them as *opportunities* for collaboration, a win-win for both sides where everybody can grow.

If you have a clearly defined brand and an awesome product, you don't have to worry about competition. Your customers and followers clearly feel connected to *you* specifically and that won't change if you share someone else's products as well.

That's why these first steps - *the 10 Sassy Questions* - are so important and why marketing will not work unless you have them in place.

You will just be spinning your wheels, wasting a lot of money and constantly fighting off competitors - not a fun way to live.

That's also why building a loyal following is so important. You will never please everybody - and you don't need to!

With 8 billion people on the planet, there are plenty of customers for everyone and if you position yourself in a unique way and care for your peeps, competition is not something you will ever have to worry much about.

Obviously, there are a few exceptions - like an almost identical "competing" product - but with common sense you should easily spot them. In most cases, peer collaborations are an awesome way to grow - and life is a lot more fun "when you are not an island"...:)

So...

Let's look now at a few strategies for effective peer collaborations:

- **Organize giveaways together** (ebooks, smaller courses) -- special sales (Black Friday) -- bundles, etc. Everyone sends an invite to their list. To access the freebies, users have to provide their email address => massive list building potential!

Since growing your following is so important, especially in the beginning, giveaways are a great way to kick start your growth.

- **YouTube collaborations:** One of the most important strategies for new YouTubers to grow. Even the big guns still do collabs as you might have noticed, because growing your audience never ends. Usually, two related videos are created with both YouTubers participating, one for each channel. Both promote to their audience, giving each other a shoutout, and the videos are usually set up as a sequence, so viewers need to watch both to get the full information.

- **Roundup Blog posts:** pick a highly shared topic or question (check Buzzsumo for ideas) and get a "roundup" of experts to give advice or answer 3 short questions.
Audiences love these posts and share them widely (viral potential).
The experts will also often share the article with their large lists, gaining you instantly more traffic - and authority by association.

- **Interviews (podcasts, blogs, Youtube):** the interviewee will usually invite their audience, driving traffic to your platform

- **Loop giveaways (Instagram)**: a group of peers and a small number of influencers form a giveaway loop. To enter the drawing, participants need to "loop" from page to page, follow each, tag a friend and usually 1-2 additional actions to qualify.

Prizes have to be valuable for people to go through the effort and should be related to your niche, so you attract new followers who are actually interested in your topic and don't just look for a free iPad...

- **Online Summits:** the latest rage and quite effective to grow your list quickly even if you are relatively new. Invite a number of bestselling authors, bloggers, podcasters or other experts to a 30 minute pre-recorded video interview. Give them a 50% affiliate link for motivation and then have everyone invite their audiences to your online summit with a small admission fee (e.g. $67). You get 50% of all sign-up fees and - even more importantly - the email address of everyone signing up. All in just a few days!

Plus, as the person running the summit, you will be seen as an industry leader and expert - even if you are brand new...

HeySummit(*) is one of the best known platforms to organize your summits.

These were some of the best known collab strategies to give you some ideas, but the sky is the limit, of course. Whatever works in your niche and with your circle of peers, always be on the lookout for ways to collaborate and leverage each others' audiences to grow your following and brand awareness.

Collab OPA is free PR(!) and can be highly effective to grow your business quickly.

Just like...

#4 - Guesting OPA

Guesting on bigger blogs, podcasts and YouTube channels is another great way to leverage other people's audiences while creating evergreen traffic streams to your brand.

Even as an online newbie you can land these gigs as long as you are an expert on your topic and have a website and offer to send them back to. An offer could be a simple lead magnet to gain subscribers for your mailing list - or, later - a free webinar that introduces your courses or services.

Podcasts and YouTube are easier to do in high numbers as you mostly just have to show up for about 30-60 minutes.

On the other hand, crafting a great blog post - *and it will need to be well written and researched to be accepted by prestigious blogs* - can take a lot more time.

Guest posts on well-known blogs and publications, however, can be a fantastic way to generate long-term, high-quality Google traffic, so both are important.

To land guest posts quickly and efficiently, I recommend Jon Morrow's training. It includes a "little black book" of editor contact info to some of the biggest blogs and publications online, sorted by genre (Forbes, Huffington Post, Fast Company, etc.).

Plus, the best in-depth training I have seen on writing marketable and high converting blog posts:

- *How to craft winning headlines (so important to draw potential readers in)*
- *How to find viral topics*
- *How to structure your posts*
- *The famous "Morrow" opening*
- *Best converting writing style*

and so much more.

Jon used to be the editor of *Copyblogger* and as such was the "gatekeeper" who decided what posts got featured - and who didn't. He is better suited than anyone to show you the insider secrets for landing high profile guest posts.

Then he started his own blog - *Smartblogger* - and grew that to 8 figures in annual revenue. *All while being paralyzed from the neck down!*

For me, it was the course that jump started my career as a writer, and it has since helped many of my students do the same who are all raving about it.

You can access it at a 30% discount here (limited time):

Jon Morrow's Guest Blogging Course(*)

#5 - Viral Blog Posts

Yup... viral....easy.... :)

While we are on the topic of guesting...

Let's have a look at blogging and whether it is still a viable marketing strategy, before you put in a lot of time and effort, expecting miracles and getting lemons.

To be honest...

These days blogging is one of the slowest, most arduous ways to grow a following and, by extension, promote a business.

Video as a content form has far overtaken blogging - both on Youtube, but also Facebook, Instagram and Twitter - and that trend will only continue to grow.

Facebook's algorithm vastly favors video content and on Instagram, videos always get a lot more engagement, tags, follows and saves.

Blogging isn't dead, but you have to be strategic and smart to gain any traction or you will be broadcasting to crickets!

Below are some of the top ways to do just that, potentially even getting a few viral moments.

Quality is once again more important than quantity here - despite what you may have heard.

Gone are the days to churn out multiple blog posts per week - or even daily. *Not* recommended anymore.

Not even for SEO purposes as Google's algorithm has become much more sophisticated at locating quality content and favors quality over repetitive, cookie-cutter "SEO posts".

Brian Dean from Backlinko is one of the most successful SEOs in the world. "SEO" stands for "search engine optimization" and is the art of ranking your content highly in Google, so potential readers can easily find you in searches.

SEO is one of the main traffic sources for blogs, which we'll discuss in a later chapter.

For our purposes here, Brian's example is fascinating, because he managed to rank for highly competitive keywords in the #1 spot, only 8 months after launching his blog Backlinko!

Unheard of!

Even more impressive:

He didn't use any black hat tactics (=semi legal/ethical back-linking strategies that most SEOs use to get to #1), but instead focused on quality content and white hat back-linking.

We'll not go into the back-linking part here, but - *more fascinatingly* - how Brian debunked the long-held belief that you need to constantly publish new content to keep the Google gods happy.

Not so at all.

He publishes roughly 1 post per month and has a total of just 30+ posts on his blog.

That's all!

Not hundreds or thousands, just 30+, but those 30+ posts are *massive* and the absolute, *ultimate* resource on their topic.

They are well written, easily 7K words, featuring videos, graphics, images, statistics and anything you could possibly want on the topic.

They are so-called "authority posts" and because they are so good - *and he can back up everything he teaches with his own phenomenal success* - thousands of other blogs started to link out to them, creating:

=> Massive back-linking power and with that
=> Massive authority with Google, which allowed him to rank for highly competitive terms like "link building" at #1 within just a few months.

Again - unheard of!

So... less is more, but make it top quality!

Not every post needs to be this extensive, but you need a few to gain traction and have people start noticing you, including influencers who can quickly put your blog "on the map" with just one tweet or shoutout!

Here is a list of the most successful blog marketing strategies - all with viral potential:

#1 - AUTHORITY POSTS

Write THE absolute authority piece on a topic. The best, most in-depth and complete piece of content available. The one that even influencers will refer to and send their audiences to. The one that easily gets shared and listed as a resource everywhere.

Not every one of your blog posts needs to be like that, of course, but even just 1 or 2 can make all the difference and drive consistent organic traffic to your blog - instantly and evergreen. Possibly for years to come.

A post *that* popular will also get a lot of love from Google and show up at the top of search results for competitive terms, even if your blog is still relatively new.

It's an absolute fast track - and most importantly, one that will keep on giving over and over again, for years to come.

A perfect blend of viral and evergreen traffic.

A widely shared authority post can also be turned into an online course with great monetization potential since you are already getting massive organic traffic that you can then funnel to your course.

#2 - ROUNDUP POSTS

A great way to connect with influencers - even some bigger names - and leverage their audience for instant traffic and recognition.

You pick a topic that's of high interest to your audience, something they are seriously struggling with and would love to get advice for from some of the top authorities in the world.

You then reach out to a number of top experts and ask them to complete a brief 1-3 question survey which will not take them more than 2-3 minutes.

Quite a few of them will gladly participate, especially once you have a bigger name or two already committed. It means minimal time input for them, but potentially free exposure to all the other experts' audiences, plus, it's prestigious to be in their company.

Always make sure there is a *win-win for everybody* involved when you want someone's collaboration, instead of hoping for a favor.

You then create a brief survey and send it to them, letting them know about your deadline and asking for their photo and relevant links (website and social media). That's mostly your entire post already!

Once the article goes live, let them know and invite them to share it with their audience, bringing you instant exposure and authority that would otherwise have taken years to build.

#3 - THE SKYSCRAPER TECHNIQUE

Developed by Brian Dean from Backlinko as a great way to quickly build quality backlinks (more on that in the **SEO chapter**) and drive traffic to your site. It works as follows:

- You research highly popular content *(Buzzsumo)*
- You make a list of blogs and brands who have featured or linked out to similar content in the past (*again Buzzsumo or a simple Google search*)
- You create a better piece of content
- You reach out to the above list and invite them to link to your article and share it.

=> Lots of quality backlinks => better Google ranking => more organic traffic to your blog

Here is a case study to make it more palatable.

#4 - REPOST ON MEDIUM
More on that in a later chapter.

#5 - PROMOTE WITH FACEBOOK ADS
More on that in a later chapter.

#6 - PROMOTE ON PINTEREST
Pinterest is for long-term evergreen traffic and **will be discussed in the next chapter.**

More blogging training:

**FREE Case Study: A Step-by-Step Guide
To Making Your Blog Posts Go Viral(*)**

**BOOK:
The Sassy Way to Starting a Successful Blog when
you have NO CLUE**

**FREE Training Webinar with Jon Morrow:
6 Figure Blogger(*)**

#6 - *Pintastic Explosion!*

It's Pinterest, y'all!

Maybe not the first marketing strategy you thought of...

But...

All the more powerful!

Especially, for evergreen - long-term - traffic.

And free at that!

Got your attention?

Pinterest is still a bit overlooked compared to Instagram, Youtube or Facebook, but definitely worth exploring.

Here are some unique features of this platform:

Pins (= Pinterest posts) are not shown in chronological order as on most other social platforms.

This means, successful pins can show at the top of search results for a long time, sometimes years. See an example here:

This image was taken in 2019 for the search term "Fitness Blog".

The top pin was originally posted in 2017!

So, even two years after its original publication, this pin is still driving massive traffic - every day - to the blog post it's pointing to.

Probably hundreds of thousands per month given how popular the topic is.

See where am I going here…?

While it takes time to gain traction on Pinterest and have your first pins go viral, once you do, those pins can keep on giving over and over - for a long time.

Not so, on Instagram or Facebook as a comparison, where chronology is the name of the game.

While influencer shoutouts can give you instant traffic and quick growth, they don't last. It's a one-off and then you need to do another.

With Pinterest, you spend a few months laying the groundwork, building up authority with the algorithm, in the hopes that eventually it will feature your content more frequently - and more prominently.

It's similar to Google in that regard and, of course, successful pins can also show high in Google searches, which can bring you even more traffic.

Search engine driven platforms aim to show their users the best suited, most relevant, high-quality content and will naturally prefer trusted sources that have proven popular with users over and over again, rather than an untested newbie.

For Pinterest that means, frequent re-pins and comments:
=> social proof, Pinterest style.

Once Pinterest starts taking you seriously and starts featuring your content on a regular basis, your pins can turn into an automatic traffic machine - all completely free!

Yes.

Free, organic - evergreen - traffic!

This can work for your blog as much as for your ecom store. For example, these two bloggers have turned their Pinterest traffic which they keep sending to their two blogs into a 100K+ monthly income - pretty much on autopilot!!

Yes, $100,000 per *month*!

And it didn't take them many years to get to that point. They started making 20K+ after just a few months.

How is that possible?

1) The blog posts that Pinterest traffic was directed to, all featured either affiliate products or their own digital products - ebooks and courses - while sharing great information that readers were highly interested in.

They became experts at researching marketable topics and crafting well-converting titles - and then put out LOTs of content.

Each blog post with multiple pins pointing at it and all pins optimized for Pinterest, meaning:

2) Keywords (=search terms) in title and description, so users could find the pins.

3) Appealing and eye-catching designs and titles, all branded, so users could easily recognize them.

4) They actively built their Pinterest following with various strategies, including group boards and Tailwind tribes.

Similar strategies will work with ecom stores, which are highly popular on Pinterest since users often come to Pinterest with the specific intention to shop!

Very different from any other social platform where ads and buy buttons are considered more of a nuisance.

If you have products to sell, especially those that lend themselves to beautiful visuals, Pinterest should be on your short list!

Again, the reminder though: focus on ONLY ONE strategy in the beginning and spend several months really mastering it, creating massive success!

Instagram or Pinterest - pick one, not both.

Each work entirely differently and will take up all your time in the beginning to get some traction.

One platform fully leveraged is more than enough to make you wealthy and even financially free over time - without spending years and thousands of dollars.

IF - you learn the ins and outs and ninja strategies that separate the 1% of successful creators from the rest.

Pinterest is no exception and will take all your time and focus in the first 3-6 months until you start seeing significant success.

The above-mentioned bloggers never focused on Instagram, YouTube or Facebook - or only minimally. They put all their *focus* on Pinterest as the main traffic source for their two blogs - and by extension their entire business - and the results were amazing.

A few more fun facts about Pinterest users:

- <u>They spend more money than any other social media platform per day</u> (even Facebook)
- In fact, people come to Pinterest specifically with the intent to BUY - *unlike other platforms where users get annoyed when they see an ad or sales offer.*
- Tend to come from a higher income bracket => more spending power
- Are college educated
- Tend to be friendlier, less trolling and nasty.
- The majority are still women although that is slowly changing.

For top-notch training, you can check out *Pinterest Avalanche* by the above mentioned two bloggers to learn all their secrets. The course is constantly updated, very reasonably priced and comes with a very active Facebook group to get all your questions answered and help along the way.

Check it out here:

PINTEREST AVALANCHE(*):
How these two bloggers turned Pinterest
into a 100k+ PER MONTH Machine
... and how YOU can do it, too!

#7 - 8 Figure Gram!

Yup - stunning, but true.

Thousands of businesses have grown from zero to 6, 7 and even 8 figures in a short amount of time, just through Instagram marketing!

In particular, influencer shoutouts.

Consultants and coaches have made tens of thousands of dollars from new clients gained through networking on Instagram!

Where Pinterest is about free, organic, *evergreen* traffic...

Instagram can give you instant gratification - though usually at a price.

Both are great platforms to massively grow a business, but are entirely different in their workings and functionality.

Pick one - not both - as each will keep you plenty busy.

To use influencer marketing for your business, you don't necessarily need a big IG page yourself as your shoutouts will redirect to your outside store or landing pages, but you might as well make use of the residual traffic and interest that will come with every shoutout and grow a noticeable presence yourself.

Plus, Instagram is transitioning into store options for business pages, similar to Pinterest and Facebook, so making it as easy as possible for potential customers to buy from you - without ever leaving the platform - is certainly a good idea.

Important to know:

Instagram went through a wave of dramatic changes in 2019 as the platform finally attempted to root out rampant cheating, automation and fake accounts.

Given the drastic algorithm changes every couple of weeks, you can now pretty much forget most of what you ever learned about growing your page on Instagram.

And it will keep changing.

What doesn't change is the importance of quality content, in this case, stunning visuals - both photos and videos.

While years ago, multiple posts per day were the way to grow fast, IG's algorithm would now perceive this as spamming and treat your page accordingly.

For a long time, you needed instant engagement within the first hour - or even the first 5-10 minutes - to get enough momentum to reach the Explore page or top spots in hashtags.

As a result, engagement groups ("pods") popped up everywhere with page owners in the same niche agreeing to post at the same time and instantly liking and commenting on each other's post, thereby triggering the algorithm and getting much higher exposure.

IG has been aggressively cracking down on engagement groups and changed the algorithm in such a way that early engagement is no longer relevant - even spammy.

Instead, slowly building momentum over 1-2 days now appears more realistic and will get more traction.

Another popular hack was "power likes & views," sold by companies who owned thousands of pages in different niches and had built them to a high follower count totaling hundreds of millions. The theory being that likes and views by a big page (aka "authority page") would be considered more important by Instagram's algorithm and therefore almost certainly get viral results for each post.

Thanks to Instagram's constant, aggressive changes throughout 2019, most of these companies are now out of business and power likes have lost much of their effectiveness.

As a result, it has become a lot more difficult to grow a page on Instagram and be seen organically, but it can certainly still be done.

Here are the two main ways to grow on Instagram quickly (and legitimately) that are unlikely to ever go out of fashion:

#1 - Influencer Shoutouts

We already discussed how influencer shoutouts work **in an earlier chapter** and I gave you a video example from *High on Life* that showed how powerful this can be in an extreme case (100K new followers in 48 ours) **- so please check that chapter for more info.**

Once again, your page needs to look amazing and have a clear branding and content strategy before you should start using influencer shoutouts - *and* - you need an amazing ad - image or video (with video usually getting a lot more engagement).

With product marketing, the influencer will often create the content, for your own page, however, it's up to you to show yourself in the most marketable way. You might want to get a professional to design and edit your ads as results can vastly improve.

#2 - Loop Giveaways

Another effective strategy that will never go out of fashion. In this case, you partner with a number of other Instagram pages, including ideally a few influencers with a large, engaged following. You offer a valuable prize that ties in with your niche, so you only attract people who will be interested in your topic (and not just that free iPad) and hopefully remain followers once the giveaway is over.

Then you tie all pages together in a loop, meaning:

1) Each page owner invites their followers to participate during a specific time frame (usually over several days).

2) Conditions to be entered in the contest include:

   * participants must follow all pages in the loop *(each page tagging the next page, so participants can easily go from one to the next)*.

   * leave a comment on the post

   * tag a friend

Or any variation thereof.

If the prize is attractive enough, you will potentially have thousands of people going through the loop - each adding to your follower count in a short amount of time.

Ads

Facebook is all about making money and the drastic changes were surely meant to also entice users to switch to IG ads for their growth. So far, they still don't seem to have nearly the same success potential as Facebook ads, but that may change over time as users get more used to seeing them in their feed.

Instagram is a complex platform and entire books and courses have been created to learn the most effective strategies. Obviously this book can only give a brief overview and touch on a few power methods to grow quickly and help you avoid wasting time.

You definitely need in-depth training if you want to use Instagram as a main marketing and income source and here are several resources to help you with that:

This is a FREE Training webinar(*) by the guys who helped giants like Gary V, Alex Becker and Kevin David grow their Instagram following quickly - and ethically (no fake followers or bots). At the end, Josue also introduces a course, but even the free part will give you some good pointers.

For **Coaches and Consultants,** you can start with my friend **Carla's FREE Instagram Bootcamp**(*). Her clients have generated 10K in revenue with just 900 followers, another leveraging 3,000 followers into 100K in consulting revenue, so another interesting option to check out.

Carla focuses on hands-on networking to find high-quality clients, so if that's your biz, she's your gal.

If you want to jump into the ring and become a **paid Instagram Influencer** yourself, **Brittany Hennessy's excellent book "Influencer"** shows you everything you need to know. Brittany is in charge of booking influencers for major marketing campaigns at Hearst Publishing. Few people are more knowledgable on the topic than she is and the book is written in a fun, entertaining way (she also reads the audiobook)…

#8 - Is Facebook still worth it?

The short answer is: Yes!

But let's look a little closer:

Facebook is still the most widely used social media platform and a great place to turn your following into an engaged community through Facebook groups.

Pretty much everyone has a Facebook profile and can be reached that way.

Any legitimate business needs a Facebook page to be taken seriously - *and* - to run Facebook Ads, which you always want as an option.

Then there are the new power players of Facebook messenger bots, which we'll talk about a little later.

So, yes. Facebook is definitely still relevant and can be an effective marketing method for your business.

Groups

Facebook groups are fantastic for community building and to interact directly with your followers, answer questions, etc. Plus, you can make them closed (highly recommended) and restrict access, giving them more of a VIP, exclusive feel.

Business Pages

In this chapter, we'll look at Facebook business pages and how you can still effectively use them.

For starters, Facebook business pages are almost impossible to grow organically and difficult to keep engagement high. Here is why:

- *Huge competition (almost everyone has a Facebook page)*

- *Due to Facebook's algorithm less than 6% of your followers actually ever get to see your daily posts!*

Yup, you didn't know that, did ya...?

So.... you posting some generic content every day or the obligatory Facebook live will usually play to crickets, because (almost) no one will see it.
- *Facebook is basically one giant competition:*

Any time you post something to your page, you are entering a competition with every other page posting at that time for a place in your followers' timeline !

Big, highly engaged pages get preference and so it's quite difficult to break through, especially in the beginning.

Why?

Obviously, Facebook wants you to buy ads, but also, because it would become overwhelming for all of us if our timelines were cluttered up with *every* post from *every* page we ever followed!

There is a good reason for this system and it rewards page owners who put in a lot of effort over time to build a highly engaged following - lots of comments, likes and shares - and weeds out pages with low quality content that rarely ever post.

In the beginning your only way to get through will be to "boost" your posts. Meaning, you pay to guarantee your post shows up in your followers' timeline.

An ad basically, that you can set up right within your post, choosing your existing followers as target audience. You can even narrow it down by location or demographics (age, gender, etc.).

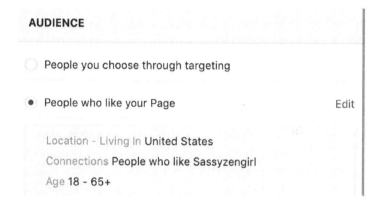

Even a $5 boost will give you significantly more - *guaranteed* - visibility and the more your followers interact with your posts, the more they will start seeing them in their timeline organically (without you having to boost). So you can improve engagement and visibility over time.

A fascinating case study for rapid growth of a Facebook page to 1 Million followers in just 30 days, can be found in this book:

1 Million Followers:
How I build a massive Social Media Following in 30 Days.

To be clear, this method requires some serious marketing dollar, but many of his principles can be helpful even if you can't spend 10K+ per month on Facebook ads.

Getting 1 Million followers to a personal brand is very difficult, no matter how big your marketing budget - so that alone is an impressive result.

To then keep those followers and turn them into an engaged, loyal following is even more impressive and this book will show you in-depth how to do it.

#9 - *Join the Tube, Baby....!*

YouTube happens to be one of my favorite platforms and I'm currently in the process of building **SassyZenGirl TV** - stay tuned...:)

It's a fantastic platform to connect with your followers and customers in a more personal way. Obviously great for tutorials and how-to's of all kinds. Great to present your expertise in a non salesy - *entertaining* - way and build a trusted following who will then also buy your products (courses, ebooks, ecom products, etc.).

Video is the leading content medium of our time, not just on YouTube, but also Facebook and Instagram, and YouTube has grown to become the top watched platform overall - with 70% of Americans watching YouTube every day!

Growing a successful YouTube channel takes time and consistent effort, but is well worth the initial effort once you start getting evergreen traffic from both Youtube *and* Google searches, which is very powerful!

YouTube is owned by Google and you have probably noticed how search results frequently feature YouTube videos - often at the very top.

There is even an entire tab on Google just for video results.

The good news:

It is much easier to get your newest YouTube video to show there than your newest blog post, because of the strong affinity and preference Google has for YouTube (and Pinterest as we saw earlier).

Again, building a YouTube presence takes a *lot* of work and long-term commitment!

You should love the medium of video and be willing to be in it for the long run.

You don't need expensive equipment to start. Your smartphone or computer camera will be just fine in the beginning, but you want to invest in a decent microphone as bad sound is the biggest turn-off for viewers - as well as good lighting.

For starters, you can use natural light sources and record next to a window for example.

You also need video editing software, because editors are expensive and you should know at least the basics and be able to do it yourself.

iMovie is a free app for Apple users and there are a few for PC/androids as well.

Take a course on **Skillshare** to learn how to use it and you'll soon be on your way.

Not rocket science!

Same goes for more advanced apps like *Adobe Premiere Pro* and Apple's *Final Cut Pro*.

As for growth strategy, here are the main factors:

1 - SEO
YouTube is a search engine, meaning people can find your channel and videos through keyword searches, so your titles and description need to be SEO optimized for easy discoverability. If SEO is completely new to you, **please read this quick beginner guide**, so you know the basic terms and

what it's all about. You will need to understand SEO, no matter what path you eventually choose - and it's much easier than it may sound right now...

2 - Thumbnails + Titles

Highly successful YouTubers always stress how extremely important thumbnails and titles are. If you look here, you can probably see why:

Your thumbnails need to stand out and "pop" - with irresistible headlines that viewers can't help but click. A major part of discoverability comes through your videos showing in "Up Next" suggestions - or a user's home page.

Thumbnail + Title is what makes people choose your video over everyone else's. Similar to books on Amazon. It's what gets people in the door.

This is why successful YouTubers will usually start each project by *first* creating title and thumbnail - and spending significant time on them - *before* they ever create the actual video! That's how important they are.

You can have the greatest video in the world, but if no one clicks on it, it's useless.

3 - Watch + Session time: Meaning the time a user spends watching any of your videos, plus all other videos afterwards, including from other channels.

In other words, the longer you keep users on YouTube, the more YouTube will "like" you and feature your videos. It is *the* most important metric of all - according to YouTube's official statements on their algorithm.

Similarly, the higher the "watch time", meaning how many minutes of your video a viewer watches before clicking on something else, the more relevant and valuable YouTube's algorithm will consider this video and show it more or less accordingly.

There are a number of strategies to increase watch + session time, which go beyond the scope of this book, but here a several resources by some of the most successful YouTube marketers that go a lot more in-depth:

BOOK:
YouTube Secrets: The Ultimate Guide to Growing Your Following and Making Money as a Video Influencer

COURSE
YouTube Growth Academy(*)

EBook
30 Days to a Better YouTube Channel(*)

Interestingly, while SEO can initially help a video rank highly and get a lot of visibility, it is ultimately the viewer response that determines a video's long-term success.

That's why watch time is so important. If users routinely click away from a video after just a few seconds, it tells YouTube that it's either low quality or not relevant to the search term.

No matter what SEO magic you might employ, your video will soon start dropping like a rock and never surface again if it gets consistently low watch time and high bounce rate.

This ensures that quality content that's *highly relevant* to the search term ("keyword") will survive and get a lot of exposure while mediocre, low quality content will disappear quickly.

That's it in a nutshell.

#10 - You've Got Mail!

Email marketing is still one of the best converting sales strategies and a must-have, no matter what type of platform or business you otherwise run.

Everyone needs to grow an active mailing list from Day 1!

Your mailing list is the *one* way you can always reliably reach your followers and customers.

You *own* your list, and you make the rules - unlike social media platforms or Amazon, Etsy, Google and the like.

Most other strategies require you to conform to the rules - *and frequent changes* - of each platform. They might even shut down at some point - or shut *you* down - , so you need at least one marketing asset that is completely in your control, that will always allow you to reach your customers and followers whenever you want.

The problem with email marketing is that people have become jaded and the tolerance level for frequent messages as well as opening rates have gone down dramatically.

How then do you build a fruitful relationship with your email subscribers?

1 - By focusing on *their* benefit first! - Your readers should look forward to hearing from you, not dreading another sales pitch.

It is totally fine to also market your products once in a while. People understand you are running a business and will support you in that - *IF* - you respect them and make it worth their while.

4 out of 5 messages should be pure benefit - the classic 80/20 rule.

Give something for free that is valuable enough for readers to open that email. Like great information, a report, case study, tip - whatever applies to your field.

Time is our most precious commodity and wasting someone's time to me is one of the most unforgivable things anyone can do.

So …

Think carefully what you send out.

<u>Would *you* enjoy reading it?</u>

Or is it just another generic talking point like most email messages these days, with everyone modeling each other's stuff and topics.

Know your audience and what they need. The better you know how to help them - or entertain them (if that's your niche) - the more readers will appreciate your mails and look forward to them.

2 - When you pitch, make it a special offer. Something you don't usually give out, something only subscribers of your list can get access to. Ideally with a time limit, so readers learn to open your mails right away.

Early Bird Specials are a particular favorite when you are about to launch a new product, an online course for example.

Advance reader copies for a book launch are another.

3 - Write as if you are telling a good friend about something. Share parts of your life, make it personal, take readers along with you.

4 - List Hygiene: we already talked about 1,000 true followers and you want to weed out your list on a regular basis - every 3-4 months:

- *Remove anyone who hasn't opened your messages in the last 4-6 months (and has been a subscriber for longer than that, of course)*
- *Remove undeliverables + unsubscribes*
- *Check Open + Clickthrough rates (CTR) on every message you send out and try to aim for at least 20% and 5% respectively. The higher the better.*

Mailing lists can get very expensive once you have a lot of subscribers (10K+), so you don't want to pay for a lot of dead weight or a vanity number with no real commercial value.

1,000 truly devoted fans that open every one of your mails and frequently buy whenever you have an offer are worth *much* more than 100,000 who barely know your name and rarely ever open your mails.

Don't let vanity numbers run your decisions. Focus on quality relationships with your readers - not quantity.

How do you get new subscribers onto your mailing list?
By offering a "lead magnet", usually a free course, checklist, case study or ebook on a topic that is highly valuable and sought after by your audience.

Something they will be *dying* to have *(hint: you need an irresistible title)*!

Valuable enough to trade their precious email address for it.

To get ideas, check out what lead magnets the top influencers in your niche use. It's obviously converting well, so you can model after that (don't copy, obviously).

With your lead magnet in place, you can link out from any of your content platforms to a "landing page" where people can give their email address in return for the promised goodie.

You need to sign up with a mailing list provider where all collected email addresses are stored and from where you can send your messages.

I use **Aweber**(*) who have greatly upped their game over the last year and are now offering all the advanced functionality of funnel, tagging and campaigns previously reserved to much more expensive platforms.

They started as more of a beginner platform a few years ago, but are now fully operational for advanced campaigns while still keeping their prices a lot lower than the competition.

They also have - by far - the best, friendliest and fastest customer support of any email platform I have seen. Chat support is usually instant (in rare cases, a few minutes) with a fully trained Aweber employee, not overseas labor that read from a script and will drive you crazy....:)

You can try them out here.(*)

This video gives you a rundown of the whole setup. It's important that you get that started as soon as possible as growing your list - and your following - should be the #1 focus from now on:

How to set up a landing page sequence in Wordpress and build your Mailing List

#11 - The most powerful Ad machine on Earth!

Facebook ads can be incredibly powerful to rapidly grow and scale your business.

However, they can also be an absolute money pit with little result and thousands of $$ wasted, so definitely not a beginner strategy - except for boosting a few posts at $5 a day.

Facebook is better than any other ad platform at laser targeting potential customers, based on every minute detail of demographics, locations, professions, interests, even income, behaviours and educational levels.

Facebook ads are truly phenomenal in that regard, but you need a decent start-up budget and thoroughly learn how to best use them.

Even then, it's a lot of testing, testing, testing - until you hit the sweet spot of positive ROI.

You should not use them for product marketing until you have all your ducks in a row, meaning:

- A professional looking landing page, optimized for conversion
- A product that your target audience really, really wants
- Great sales copy, both for the ad and the landing page
- Eye-catching visuals

Creating a great ad and learning all the ins and outs of Facebook targeting, will do nothing if your backend is not in tip-top shape!

<u>Really take note of this</u> or you will be wasting a *lot* of money with little result!

To get your feet wet - as you will certainly use Facebook ads on a larger scale eventually - I recommend starting with a few boosts.

Yes, boosts don't have the full targeting functionality, as the gurus will complain, but they are far less confusing and you can't lose a lot of money if you run them for a day or two at $5 a day - as an example.

Here is another way that can work great for beginners without breaking the bank:

Promote popular Blog Posts

This is something I learned from Monica Louie and her excellent course. She teaches bloggers to promote their blog posts at minimal expense - 6c per click!

The posts can, of course, contain affiliate offers or lead to other product sales, so there is a way to make this small investment back - and then some!

More importantly though, it is a very effective way to drive traffic to your blog and get new subscribers quickly - especially when you are brand new and struggling to get an audience.

This will only work though *(once again)* if you have your backend in order:

You need high converting, *irresistible* headlines (so be sure to **study and apply Headline Hacks in-depth(*))** as well as eye-catching images that capture people's attention in their busy feed.

If you want to check out Monica's training, you can do so here (I'm not an affiliate). Again, this is specific for blogging though the same principles apply to ecom, books and other offers. I've successfully used her strategies to market webinars and courses. They work.

Monica Louie: Flourish with Facebook Ads

And here is one of the best known courses on Facebook ads, which only opens a few times per year:

Rick Mulvaney: Facebook Ads Foundations

#12 - Messenger Bots: The cool, new Kids on the Block

Facebook messenger chatbots are the latest rage and have proven highly successful in increasing sales conversions and lead generation.

With a staggering 60-80% opening rate and 10-20% click-through rate, this is definitely a strategy you want to keep an eye on and possibly incorporate down the road.

Rather than a long-winded explanation, I invite you to watch this awesome example of a highly effective chatbot. You'll easily see why bots are so powerful and how much potential they have - for *any* niche or objective.

Gary V's VIP Messenger Bot

Pretty awesome, huh...?

Aside from impressive results, messenger bots also bring the response time of your Facebook business/

store page to "instant". This is an important parameter when Facebook evaluates your page and can improve your overall visibility as well as post reach. (= **how many of your followers get to see your posts organically**).

Plus, messenger bots allow you to easily reach all your subscribed followers with a quick blast or group message while your regular posts have a reach of less than 6% **as we discussed earlier**.

Here are some more marketing needs where messenger bots can be highly effective:

- *Quickly help new visitors find what they are looking for and what your brand offers*

- *Qualify your visitors with an engaging two-way conversation, so you can tailor your marketing according to their specific needs & preferences*

- *VIP treatment. Share insider knowledge that's only available via chat.*

- *Book appointments*

- *Highlight promotions and special offers/discounts*

- *Make checkout more engaging*

- *Get customer feedback & surveys*

- *Send order updates & event reminders*

- *Provide 24/7 access to FAQs*

- *Drip content (for example, lead magnet)*

and many more. The sky is the limit really.

One of the most versatile chatbot options is **MobileMonkey and you can test it out for FREE right here(*).**

Messenger bots are easy to set up and allow you to mimic your brand personality as you saw in Gary V's example.

The bot can talk as you or as an imaginary assistant - have fun with it...:)

Messenger bots can make interactions a lot more fun and entertaining for your customers, rather than the usual, boring onboarding experience.

MobileMonkey also partnered with one of the top marketing agencies in the US - AdVenture Media and their CEO Isaac Rudansky - who've had amazing success using chatbots with many of their top level clients.

Isaac's inexpensive Udemy course takes you in-depth into all the ins and outs of messenger bots (using MobileMonkey) with specific case studies for different uses (coaching, consulting, ecommerce, local businesses), scripts, sales psychology, etc.

You can check it out here(*).

#13 - Medium: Blogging on Steroids

Medium is another newer marketing option that most entrepreneurs are not incorporating yet.

Given the vast reach of this platform and an algorithm that favors quality content over pedigree or social media following of its authors, it's a great platform to start blogging when you have no following yet.

An expertly trained editorial team is always on the lookout for the most interesting articles on any given topic, regardless of how new or well-known the writer is. Even as a complete newbie you have a reasonable chance to have your content featured to a wider audience and start growing a following.

How do you get seen on Medium?

...among the millions of users.

Medium's algorithm is focused on quality first and foremost. Posts are not shared chronologically as would be typical on blogs and most social media platforms, but rather by quality and popularity. Quite similar to Pinterest's algorithm in that regard.

Ranking factors include:

- Whether a post has been *read* (vs. just the number of clicks)
- Whether people click the "**Recommend**" button at the bottom
- The **ratio** of people who **view it and also read it**
- As well as the **ratio** of those who **read it and also recommend it**

This approach helps level the playing field regardless of someone's following and gives everyone a fair chance to stand out.

Getting other users to recommend your articles is the most important factor, especially in the first 24 hours.

If you get at least 200 hearts in that time frame, you have a good chance of getting included in "Top Stories of the Day", which are featured prominently on the website and app as well as in daily emails, potentially giving you a massive boost in visibility.

To jump start the process you can promote your post with Facebook ads to get that initial boost - or - if you already have a mailing list or social media following, share it with your fans and ask them to recommend it.

Medium's homepage features three areas:

1) Your reading list *(content recommended by Medium based on the collections and people you follow)*
2) Your bookmarks
3) The Top 100 most read posts from the current month

Collections

A great way to quickly get more exposure is to submit your content to relevant "collections". These are curated by Medium users and require vetting and approval, so once again, quality is king.

Publications

Similar to collections, you can start your own publication and feature other writers as well. Conversely, as a new writer on Medium, you can ask other publications to include your stories and get more exposure that way.

How to use Medium to promote your Business?

Not by pitching and talking only about your products *(obviously...)*.

Rather, as with all content platforms, provide top-notch content around your niche and establish yourself as a thought leader in your field.

Create collections around certain topics and start recommending articles to people who follow you and your collections.

To Blog or Not to Blog?

You can either amplify your blog posts by reposting them on Medium - or - replace your blog altogether.

The latter is not ideal, because it's still important to have one platform that you own, even if your blog doesn't have the same reach and authority as Medium.

Here are two helpful articles by Larry Kim with tips on how to succeed on Medium as well as one article on using tags:

10 Insanely Good Reasons you should publish on Medium
7 Medium Optimization Tips to get your Articles to go Hot
Medium Tagging Tips

#14 - SEO (Platform Specific)

SEO is the bread and butter of online marketing. No matter what platform or strategy you decide to focus on, you still need to understand and apply the principles of SEO, not just for your website, but for any other algorithm-based platform.

Meaning a platform that functions as a search engine = you enter a search term *(= keyword)* and the algorithm returns what it thinks are the best suited results for you.

We've all been there, right...?

Amazon, eBay, Etsy, Pinterest, YouTube and, of course, Google all are SEO based search engines.

SEO stands for "search engine optimization" and is the art or science of optimizing your content or product pages in such a way that they can easily be found by anyone searching for related terms.

In this chapter, we will focus on Google SEO, which concerns your website or blog and to some degree also YouTube videos and Pinterest pins since they, too, can rank highly in Google.

If SEO is a completely new concept to you, don't worry...:) - I wrote a brief beginner guide in the *"Sassy...No CLUE!"* series just for that purpose **and you can get it here**:

In a nutshell, SEO is about creating *the appearance of authority and relevance* in the eyes of Google. The more important and relevant Google considers your posts or website, the higher it will rank your content for relevant search terms.

Obviously, your website will never reach the authority of sites like Amazon, CNN, Wikipedia or TripAdvisor to name just a few random examples - no matter what strategies you use.

So super general terms like "travel" "politics" "weight loss" will always be out of reach.

Instead, it's much more effective to target so-called "long tail keywords", meaning phrases that are more defined and specific. For example:

How to travel the world for $10 a day
Best Street Food in Chiang Mai in August
Weight loss Tips for pregnant women with diabetes

Far fewer people will "target" (= try to rank for) those specific phrases and as long as enough people are searching for them - aka "search volume" - you can receive a decent amount of traffic to your website and generate consistent sales without much effort or expense.

Other than optimizing your content for SEO by placing relevant keywords in headlines, sub heads, image ALT text and body text, how do you make your site more authoritative?

Especially, in a short amount of time?

The magic word is "backlink", meaning:

How many websites are linking to your site and how authoritative are they?

If the New York Times or Vanderbilt University link to you, it will instantly boost your site's credibility and authority, while the brand new site of your friend won't have much effect. And you certainly don't want any scam sites linking to you - bad, bad, bad... *(btw, always delete comment spam like car insurance quotes and other garbage links from your blog, as they can really harm your Google reputation).*

The name of the game when it comes to Google SEO is high-quality backlinks and gradually building more and more over time.

Entire courses and books have been created about SEO, so I won't attempt to explain it any more in this short format. Instead, here are a few resources to take your SEO game to the next level:

Sassy...NO CLUE Beginner Guide

Best SEO Blog:
Backlinko

Best SEO Course:
SEO That Works

SEO can send you free evergreen traffic for years to come - similar in that regard to Pinterest, except it takes a lot more consistent effort and link building to get to that point.

If you want to focus on SEO, I recommend going through Brian's super in-depth, free articles

(**Backlinko**) and - if you can - invest in his course (**SEO That Works**). I'm not an affiliate, but can 100% vouch, that it is the best SEO course available - and one of the very few that do not use black hat tactics that can get you banned or often don't survive during the next Google update that will surely come (*so* many sites have been ruined by this...).

#15 - Podcasting

Podcasts have been exploding in recent years and popularity is constantly rising with 24% of Americans listening to podcasts every month!

Yup.... that's a quarter of the population!

As a marketing tool, podcasts can provide you with the following benefits:

- You are reaching an on-the-go audience who may not have the time or patience to read through an article or watch a video. Plus, many people have lengthy commutes and like passing the time with a good podcast.

- Almost everyone has access to podcasts via their smartphone and most modern cars are equipped to access podcasts very easily.

- Listening to your voice can build trust and is more personal than just reading words on a page.

Podcasting provides you with an additional way to connect with your audience in a more intimate setting.

- You can continue to position yourself as an expert and thought leader in your niche. *Having your own podcast lends prestige and class to your brand.*

- Podcast directories offer another opportunity for exposure and brand awareness to people who may have otherwise never heard of you

- Your own podcast can be an excellent way to connect with influencers, even bigger names, when you invite them to be interviewed. Plus, it's a great way to leverage their audience as they will usually share and invite their audience when the episode goes live. Remember OPA?

- Recording a podcast episode will take significantly less time than writing a high-quality blog post, especially once you've had some practice. It's also far less techie and time intensive than editing and recording a video on YouTube.

Getting a podcast off the ground and finding an audience takes a lot of work initially, of course - unless you already have an audience in place.

You need to learn the top strategies of ranking on iTunes, Stitcher and other platforms, so new listeners can easily find you.

If you want to explore this option further, I recommend starting with John Lee Dumas' FREE Course.

JLD, from the top ranked "Entrepreneur on Fire" podcast, is one of the best known business podcasters and can show you all the Ninja hacks and strategies you need, to quickly gain traction and grow a successful podcast with an engaged audience.

He built his platform from zero to a steady 6 figures income per month(!) in just a few years and can best explain how to leverage a podcast to market your business and grow brand awareness:

FREE Podcast Course(*)
with John Lee Dumas

What now...?

There you have it!

An overview of the 15 most effective marketing strategies today, with the basics on how each works and what experience level is required to get started.

You also got an introduction into copywriting and sales funnels.

Most importantly, you learned what should be *your #1 most important task* to focus on over the next year and beyond: growing a loyal following.

You answered the 10 Sassy Questions to set yourself up for success from the start.
And you will not just throw out ideas and hope some will stick!

Nope!

You will have a clear strategy:

From finding highly attractive and marketable products...

To finding your sub-niche and specific audience.

With an easy-to-understand - *fun* - laser targeted message to instantly explain what you do and what your brand is all about.

And...

You are well on your way to designing an *irresistible* brand that customers will love to follow and buy from.

You are all set, my friend!

Now you just have to go out and actually DO IT!

Which is where most people stop.

But...

Not you!

YOU are a go-getter and can't wait to get started and crush it!

Right...?

And.....

#ShareYourAWESOME with the world, one special product at a time!

I wish you all the very best on this amazing journey and am always available to answer questions **in our friendly Facebook group - which you can join right here**.

To Your Success!!

Warmest regards,

Gundi Gabrielle
SassyZenGirl.com
SassyZenGirl.TV
SassyZenGirl.Store

Award Winning
INFLUENCER FAST TRACK
Series

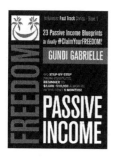

#1 Bestselling
BEGINNER INTERNET MARKETING
Series
"The Sassy Way... when you have NO CLUE!"

#1 Bestselling
TRAVEL BOOKS

Score FREE Flights, Rental
Cars & Accommodations.
Dramatically reduce Airfares.
Get paid to Travel & START a
DIGITAL NOMAD BIZ
you can run from anywhere
in the world!

**ZEN TRAVELLER
BALI**
A QUICK GUIDE

Explore the "real" Bali…
The quiet, magical parts
far away from the
tourist crowds…

More SassyZenGirl Yummies

COURSES

SassyZenGirl's Blogging Bootcamp
SassyBlogBootcamp.com

FREE Masterclass:
100K BESTSELLER BLUEPRINT
100KBestseller.com

About the Author

Gundi Gabrielle, aka *SassyZenGirl*, is an Award Winning, Top 100 Business Author and Founder/CEO of SassyZenGirl - #ClaimYourFREEDOM, a platform that helps newbie entrepreneurs turn their passion into a thriving business.

Gundi loves to explain complex matters in an easy to understand, fun way. Her *"The Sassy Way...when you have NO CLUE!!"* series has helped thousands around the world conquer the jungles of internet marketing with humor, simplicity and some sass.

A 13-time #1 Bestselling Author, Entrepreneur and former Carnegie Hall conductor, Gundi employs marketing chops from all walks of life and loves to help her readers achieve their dreams in a practical, fun way. Her students have published multiple #1 Bestsellers outranking the likes of Tim Ferris, John Grisham, Hal Elrod and Liz Gilbert.

When she is not writing books or enjoying a cat on her lap (or both), she is passionate about exploring the world as a Digital Nomad, one awesome adventure at a time.

She has no plans of settling down anytime soon.

SassyZenGirl.com
SassyZenGirl.Group
SassyZenGirl.Store
100KBestseller.com
SassyZenGirl.TV

Instagram.com/SassyZenGirl
Facebook.com/SassyZenGirl
Twitter.com/SassyZenGirl
Pinterest.com/SassyZenGirl

Made in the USA
San Bernardino, CA
12 May 2020